KENDAL

A HISTORY AND CELEBRATION
OF THE TOWN

ARTHUR NICHOLLS & TREVOR HUGHES

Produced by The Francis Frith Collection
exclusively for

OTTAKAR'S

www.ottakars.co.uk

First published in the United Kingdom in 2005
by The Francis Frith Collection®

Hardback Edition 2005
ISBN 1-84567-748-X

British Library Cataloguing in Publication Data

Kendal - A History and Celebration of the Town
Arthur Nicholls & Trevor Hughes

The Francis Frith Collection
Frith's Barn, Teffont,
Salisbury, Wiltshire SP3 5QP
Tel: +44 (0) 1722 716 376
Email: info@francisfrith.co.uk
www.francisfrith.co.uk

Printed and bound in England

Front Cover: **KENDAL, MARKET PLACE 1924** 75795t

Additional modern photographs by Trevor Hughes.

Domesday extract used in timeline by kind permission of
Alecto Historical Editions, www.domesdaybook.org
Aerial photographs reproduced under licence from
Simmons Aerofilms Limited.
Historical Ordnance Survey maps reproduced under licence from
Homecheck.co.uk

Every attempt has been made to contact copyright holders of
illustrative material. We will be happy to give full acknowledgement in
future editions for any items not credited. Any information should be
directed to The Francis Frith Collection.

*The colour-tinting in this book is for illustrative purposes only,
and is not intended to be historically accurate*

Contents

KENDAL FROM THE AIR 1929 AF26580

Historical Timeline for Kendal

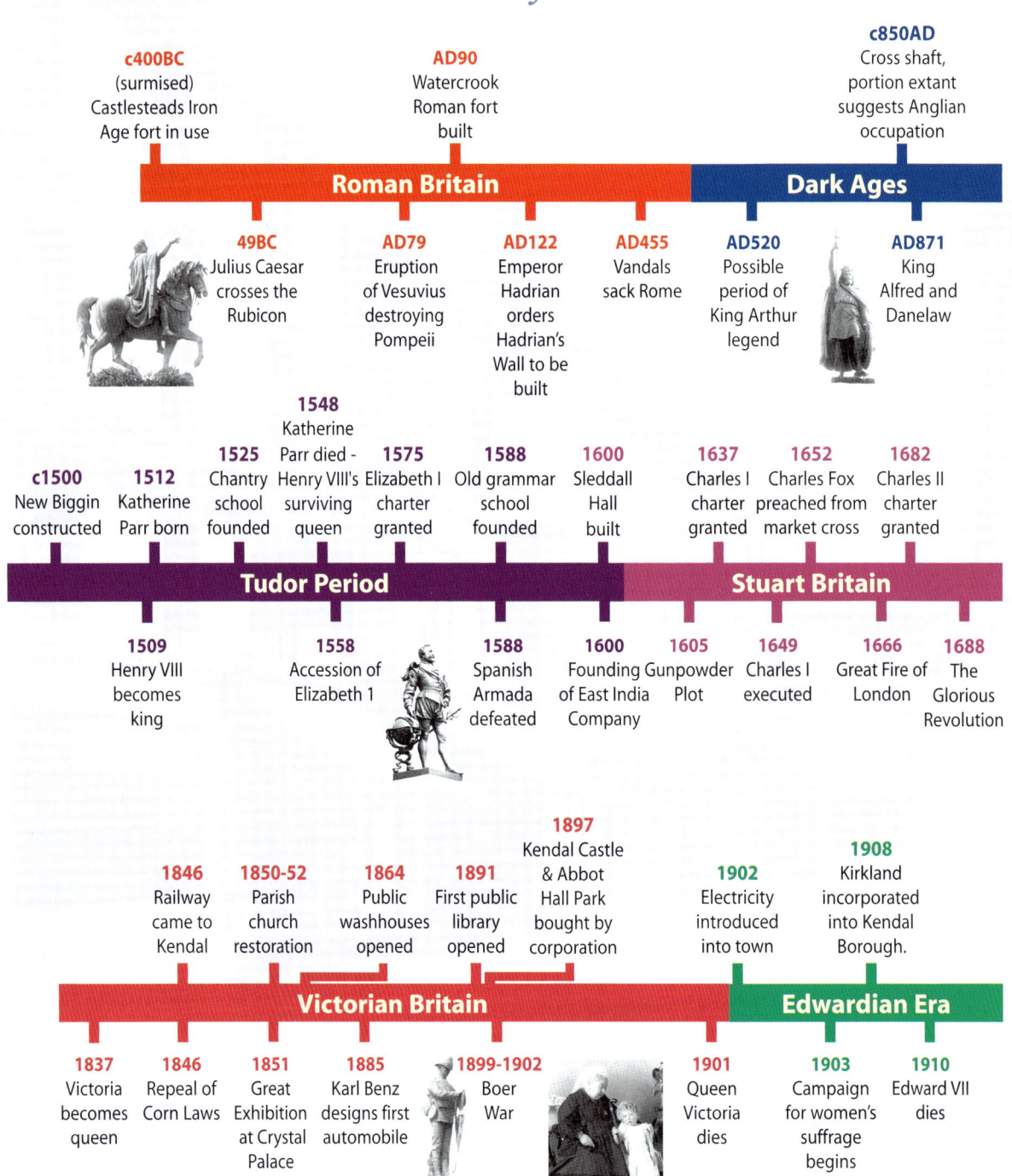

c400BC
(surmised)
Castlesteads Iron
Age fort in use

AD90
Watercrook
Roman fort
built

c850AD
Cross shaft,
portion extant
suggests Anglian
occupation

Roman Britain | Dark Ages

49BC
Julius Caesar
crosses the
Rubicon

AD79
Eruption
of Vesuvius
destroying
Pompeii

AD122
Emperor
Hadrian
orders
Hadrian's
Wall to be
built

AD455
Vandals
sack Rome

AD520
Possible
period of
King Arthur
legend

AD871
King
Alfred and
Danelaw

c1500
New Biggin
constructed

1512
Katherine
Parr born

1525
Chantry
school
founded

1548
Katherine
Parr died -
Henry VIII's
surviving
queen

1575
Elizabeth I
charter
granted

1588
Old grammar
school
founded

1600
Sleddall
Hall
built

1637
Charles I
charter
granted

1652
Charles Fox
preached from
market cross

1682
Charles II
charter
granted

Tudor Period | Stuart Britain

1509
Henry VIII
becomes
king

1558
Accession of
Elizabeth 1

1588
Spanish
Armada
defeated

1600
Founding
of East India
Company

1605
Gunpowder
Plot

1649
Charles I
executed

1666
Great Fire of
London

1688
The
Glorious
Revolution

1897
Kendal Castle
& Abbot
Hall Park
bought by
corporation

1846
Railway
came to
Kendal

1850-52
Parish
church
restoration

1864
Public
washhouses
opened

1891
First public
library
opened

1902
Electricity
introduced
into town

1908
Kirkland
incorporated
into Kendal
Borough.

Victorian Britain | Edwardian Era

1837
Victoria
becomes
queen

1846
Repeal of
Corn Laws

1851
Great
Exhibition
at Crystal
Palace

1885
Karl Benz
designs first
automobile

1899-1902
Boer
War

1901
Queen
Victoria
dies

1903
Campaign
for women's
suffrage
begins

1910
Edward VII
dies

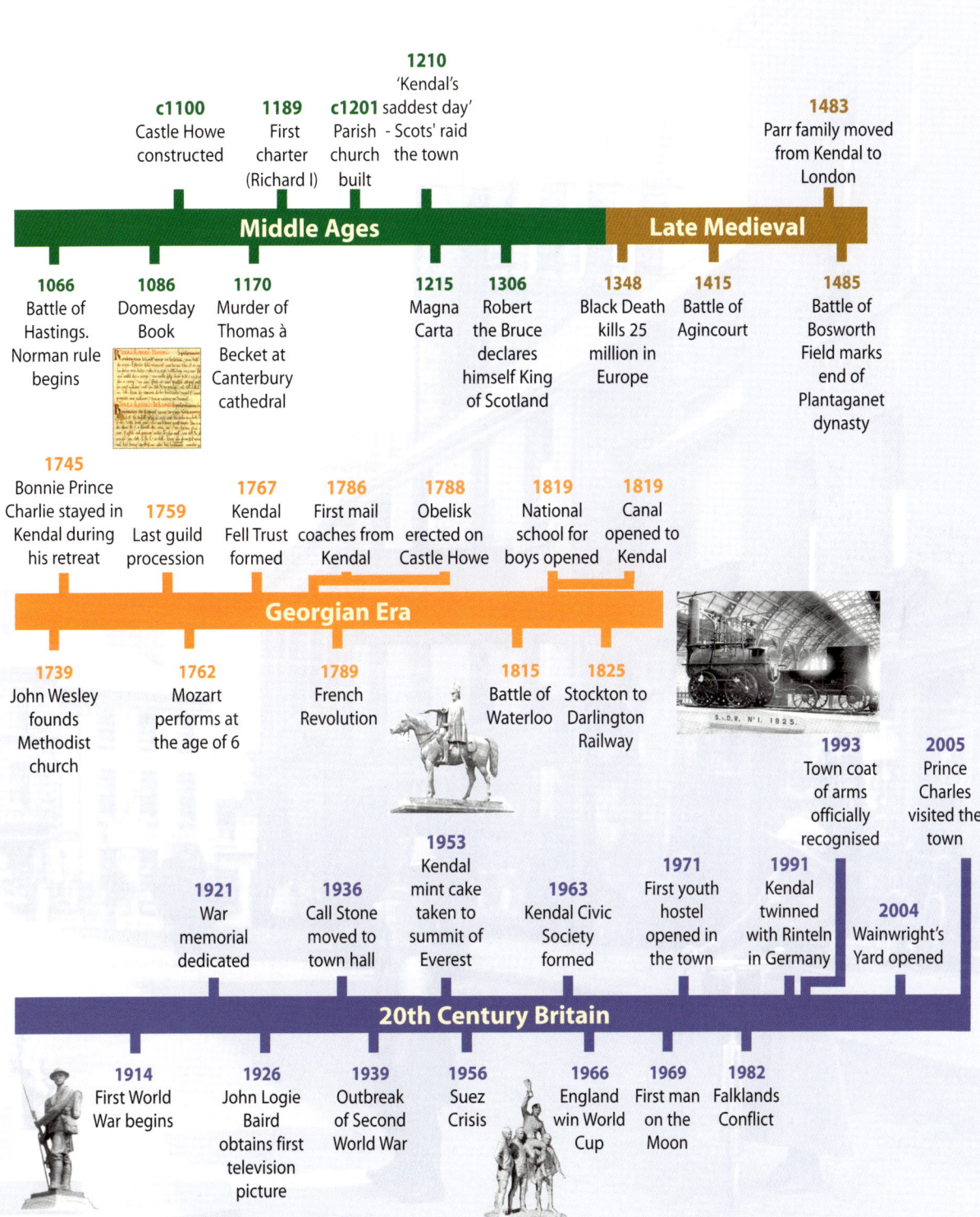

1210
'Kendal's saddest day' - Scots' raid the town

c1100
Castle Howe constructed

1189
First charter (Richard I)

c1201
Parish church built

1483
Parr family moved from Kendal to London

Middle Ages

Late Medieval

1066
Battle of Hastings. Norman rule begins

1086
Domesday Book

1170
Murder of Thomas à Becket at Canterbury cathedral

1215
Magna Carta

1306
Robert the Bruce declares himself King of Scotland

1348
Black Death kills 25 million in Europe

1415
Battle of Agincourt

1485
Battle of Bosworth Field marks end of Plantaganet dynasty

1745
Bonnie Prince Charlie stayed in Kendal during his retreat

1759
Last guild procession

1767
Kendal Fell Trust formed

1786
First mail coaches from Kendal

1788
Obelisk erected on Castle Howe

1819
National school for boys opened

1819
Canal opened to Kendal

Georgian Era

1739
John Wesley founds Methodist church

1762
Mozart performs at the age of 6

1789
French Revolution

1815
Battle of Waterloo

1825
Stockton to Darlington Railway

1993
Town coat of arms officially recognised

2005
Prince Charles visited the town

1953
Kendal mint cake taken to summit of Everest

1921
War memorial dedicated

1936
Call Stone moved to town hall

1963
Kendal Civic Society formed

1971
First youth hostel opened in the town

1991
Kendal twinned with Rinteln in Germany

2004
Wainwright's Yard opened

20th Century Britain

1914
First World War begins

1926
John Logie Baird obtains first television picture

1939
Outbreak of Second World War

1956
Suez Crisis

1966
England win World Cup

1969
First man on the Moon

1982
Falklands Conflict

KENDAL

An Introduction

AN AERIAL VIEW OF THE TOWN 1965 ZZZ04096 (Trevor Hughes Collection)

SOMEONE IN THE RECENT PAST dreamed up the title for Kendal, 'Gateway to the Lake District', and so it is, and in its unassuming way the town has seen the masses passing through on their way to the delights of the fells, missing the attractions of a wonderful town.

Kendal has a long, rich and stimulating history. Its origins go back to prehistoric times. Its story encompasses life in all its compelling aspects and its future is one to be contemplated with eager delight. Many are the famous and the fascinating people who have trod its streets, adding to the rich tapestry of our nation's story. Kendal's buildings demonstrate its importance as a thriving market town over the centuries. Kendal mint cake is known world-wide, even to the heights of Mount Everest.

This book is dedicated to those nameless men, women and children, past and present, who have given so much to make Kendal a town of which to be proud and for generations to come to cherish, and to those who carry on its rich traditions.

OPPOSITE: THE PARISH CHURCH 1896 38532

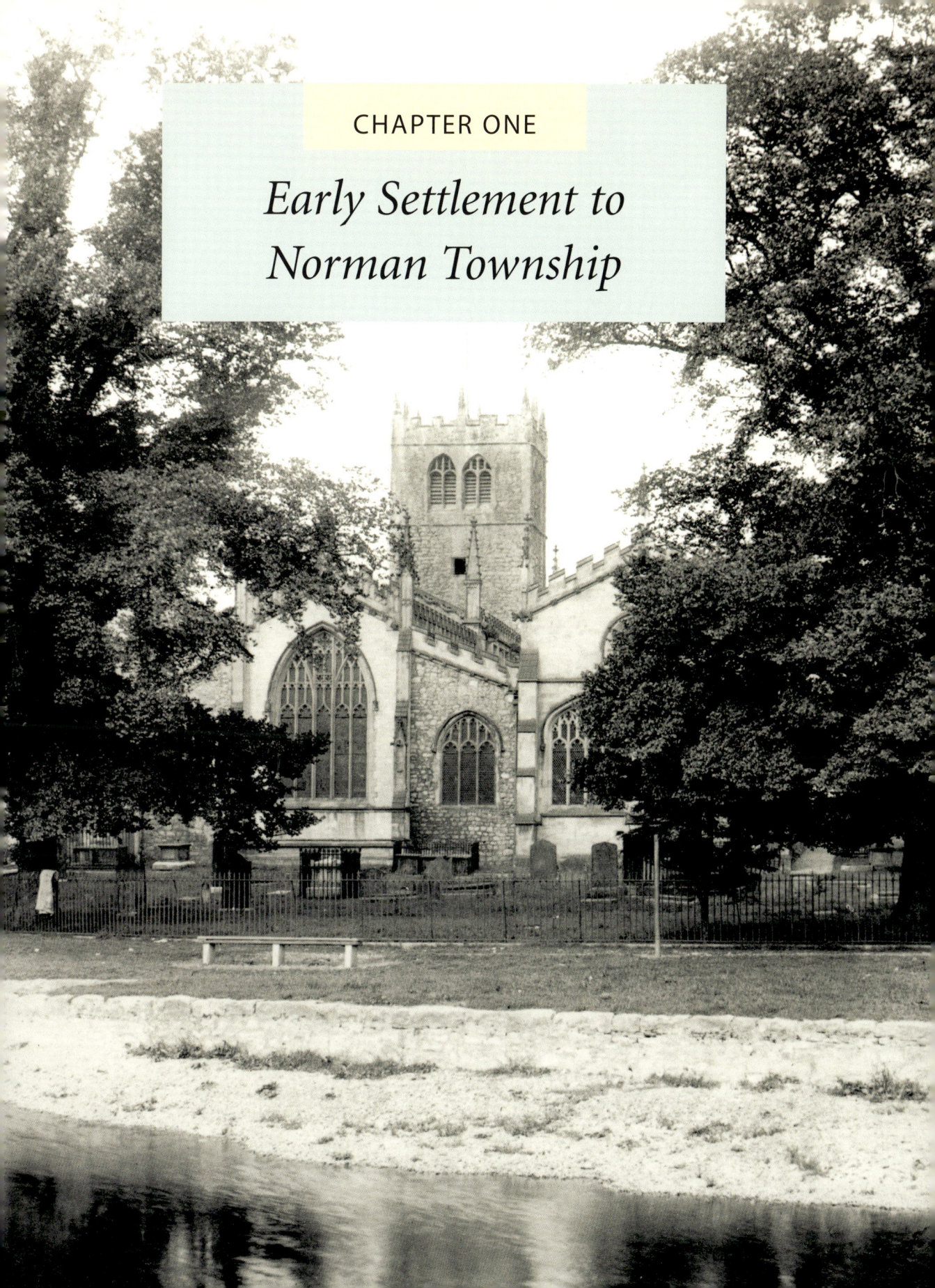

CHAPTER ONE

Early Settlement to Norman Township

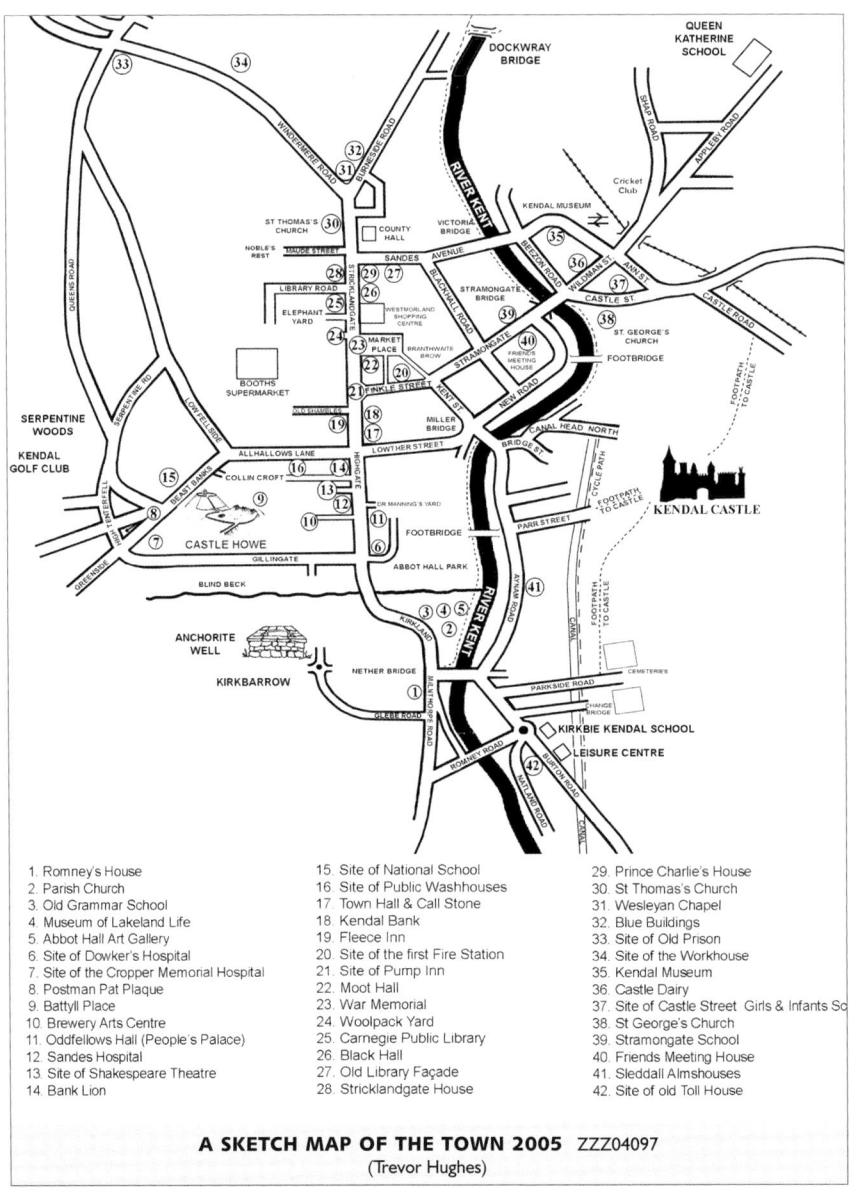

1. Romney's House
2. Parish Church
3. Old Grammar School
4. Museum of Lakeland Life
5. Abbot Hall Art Gallery
6. Site of Dowker's Hospital
7. Site of the Cropper Memorial Hospital
8. Postman Pat Plaque
9. Battyll Place
10. Brewery Arts Centre
11. Oddfellows Hall (People's Palace)
12. Sandes Hospital
13. Site of Shakespeare Theatre
14. Bank Lion

15. Site of National School
16. Site of Public Washhouses
17. Town Hall & Call Stone
18. Kendal Bank
19. Fleece Inn
20. Site of the first Fire Station
21. Site of Pump Inn
22. Moot Hall
23. War Memorial
24. Woolpack Yard
25. Carnegie Public Library
26. Black Hall
27. Old Library Façade
28. Stricklandgate House

29. Prince Charlie's House
30. St Thomas's Church
31. Wesleyan Chapel
32. Blue Buildings
33. Site of Old Prison
34. Site of the Workhouse
35. Kendal Museum
36. Castle Dairy
37. Site of Castle Street Girls & Infants School
38. St George's Church
39. Stramongate School
40. Friends Meeting House
41. Sleddall Almshouses
42. Site of old Toll House

A SKETCH MAP OF THE TOWN 2005 ZZZ04097
(Trevor Hughes)

WE CAN ONLY DEDUCE the earliest history of Kendal from the occasional finds unearthed by chance. A stone axe and a quern for grinding corn have been found in excavations in the centre of town, traces of a Bronze-Age burial site on its southern edge, and animal bones all give clues to life here in days before written history. Kendal's oldest historic site dates from prehistoric times, a place now known as the Anchorite Well, situated in the present housing estate of Kirkbarrow which rises moderately above Kirkland. The well is filled by a stream arising in the fell above and running down to the river. It has

THE ANCHORITE WELL 2005 K4701k (Trevor Hughes)

the property, even in the parched summer weather, of never running dry. This quality might have engendered an atmosphere of magic or awe resulting in a form of worship of the earth-mother goddess. A colony of sorts was established in the south-eastern facing hollow around the holy well and here seems to have been the origin of the town. Christianity came to Kendal, whether with the Romans or later through Celtic missionaries, in the 6th or 7th centuries, and the well became, through simple transliteration, dedicated to St Mary (mother of God) and a church was

raised there, remaining until the Reformation. When the present parish church was built the old church was left as a chantry. In a list of chantries in the 16th century it was recorded as Tholdwork or The Old Work or The Old Building and was eventually taken down. The well itself suffered dereliction from the 1930s but has since been restored. It now stands in private land in front of housing, but can be glimpsed through a gate.

At some time people settled beside the clean, swift-flowing river to found a community in the valley warmed by the Gulf Stream in

A RECONSTRUCTION OF AN IRON AGE ROUNDHOUSE
ZZZ01297 (Reproduced by kind permission of the
Ancient Technology Centre, Cranborne, Dorset)

Morecambe Bay. The area we now know as Westmorland was part of the populous nation of the Brigantes, the last of the tribes to submit to Roman rule. These early settlers were cattle farmers. This is remembered in the name Stricklandgate in the northern part of the town, from Stirkland, recorded as Stercland in the Domesday Book, being a pasture land for cattle. Stricklandgate was the road along which the young cattle were driven to the stirk-lands where they pastured in common.

To the south of the town, above the village of Oxenholme, is the site of the ancient hill fort of Castlesteads on the summit of the prominent hill, The Helm, from

Watercrook

The story of the Roman fort of Medibogdu (Watercrook) is shrouded in mystery.

It was set up around AD90, in a bow of the River Kent with the protection of water on three sides, as part of a chain of garrisons for patrolling and policing Cumbria. Although there are no recorded battles, the army had to be vigilant: The tombstone of the officer Flavius Romanus, now housed in Kendal Museum, shows that he was actually killed inside the fort and that part of the Twentieth Legion (Valeria Victrix) may have been stationed there. The Legion's departure would have been a social and economic disaster for those who depended on it for their livelihood.

AN ARTIST'S IMPRESSION OF A ROMAN HELMET FOUND IN GERMANY
ZZZ01293

THE SITE OF WATERCROOK ROMAN FORT
1949 ZZZ04098 (Trevor Hughes Collection)

which extensive views can be had over the surrounding countryside in all directions. It is possible that this fort was constructed by a local group of the Brigantes, called the Setantii by the classical writer Ptolemy, and that it was later used by the all-conquering Romans as a signal station before they built their fort at Watercrook.

The land around the fort was gradually opened up to arable farming and a thriving civilian population grew up around it to serve the military needs. From this it is certain that a market was formed and as Kendal became the hub of Roman roads leading in many directions trade would have been brought to the settlement. The indigenous community to some extent became integrated with its over-rulers and gained from their protection. This aptitude has enabled the people of Kendal to adapt to change. The Roman occupation ended in the 4th century and the Dark Ages of some 600 years began. The fort disintegrated over time and disappeared from sight, only to be discovered by modern archaeology. It is on private land and little can now be seen. The Romans came, saw, and left little trace of their presence.

Almost nothing is known about the beginnings of the town in these troubled times but, again, there are clues. That a community

The limestone escarpment looks over the Lyth Valley, famous for damsons. The old racecourse was on the south-eastern side. The domed shelter on the skyline, called The Mushroom, was built to mark the coronation of King George V in 1910. It contains a panorama of the surrounding views.

SCOUT SCAR 1896 38539

developed on the road between Watercrook and the nearby village of Natland is indicated by the name of the lost river crossing of Bodelford (Bothelford) and by the Viking place names that still exist, such as 'gate' for street as in Stricklandgate and Soutergate, and 'beck' for a stream. The Brigante people, having lived under Roman subjugation, were an easy prey to later invaders. The Norse Vikings came up from Morecambe Bay and set about in their customarily energetic way to clear spaces in the surrounding forests to form clearings or thwaites, another Viking name still to be found in the town, such as Branthwaite Brow in its very centre.

The Angles and Saxons came and made their transient mark. Although no trace at all has ever been found, it is thought by many that the Saxons planted a church with a thatched roof and wattle and mud-daubed walls by the side of the River Kent, under the charge of a resident priest. Some support for this conjecture comes from the naming of the town as 'Cherchebi' in Domesday Book and that the Normans subsequently built a new church, the present parish church, on the site or in the close vicinity. Some red sandstone found in parts of today's church is thought to be of Saxon origin. The small town grew up around the church, taking in the earlier settlement in the vicus of the Roman fort, and included in its name that of the river, originally named the Cam and later changed to Ken. The town became known by the succeeding Angles as Kirk byre Can dale – the Church town on the Cam (or in Kent dale). There is evidence of monastic preaching

THE RIVER KENT NORTH OF THE TOWN 1921   70686

crosses in villages around Kendal and there might well have been one in the churchyard – who knows? A small piece of the shaft of an Anglian cross, which was found built into the fabric of the church, is preserved on a window-sill in the Parr Chapel and is dated AD850. When first exhibited it was placed upside down! It is one of the very few artefacts from such an early time. Kendal showed from early days its resilience, as it suffered the advance of the Romans, their retreat, the invasions of the Picts, and the harrying of the Danes and the Saxons, winning through to build up its community slowly and steadily into one of strong character and wealth through trade.

The coming of the Normans began another phase in the life of the town and from this point we have the beginning of written records to flesh out the story of Kendal. Notable of these is the famous Domesday Book (or Book of Judgement). This was not a religious tract but was the record of a great survey of his newly acquired lands ordered by William the Conqueror and completed in 1086. According to the Anglo Saxon Chronicle it documented details of the size and nature of the land held by the lordship and his vassals, the number of villagers, cottagers and slaves, the number of ploughs held and, most significantly, what it was all worth in military terms and in taxation.

As a result of the Normans' devastation of the unruly northern counties and the fact that the Scottish kingdom of Strathclyde reached into them, the survey only included the southern part of Westmorland which included Stercaland (Strickland), an area of 20 carucates (hides or ploughs) amounting to 2,400 acres of taxable land occupied by one Gillmichael. In this land were the lost ford of Bodelford (Bothelford) over the River Kent between Natland and Helsington, and Cherchebi which was our Kendal. Who Gillmichael might have been is lost in history; he was probably the local feudal landowner. One of William's early acts was to establish a system of baronies and to replace the existing local land lords with the most favoured of his followers, the land being held by the Crown and conferred on them with the reservation of stated services and payments. The barons were men of great power but under royal control. Cherchebi was conferred on Ivo de Tailebois of the French House of Anjou, who was living in Lincoln and whose marriage to Lucy, the sister of the Saxon earls, Edwin and Morcar, was instrumental in his becoming the first Baron of Kendal – as we will now call the town.

The Normans set up castles with some speed at strategic or in other ways important sites all over the country, and one such was raised on a rocky hill to the west of the town, known today as Castle Howe. It was probably placed there more to guard against Scottish raiders than to dominate the town, which it certainly did to show that the baron held control over the inhabitants. The mound on which it was built and the adjoining flat open space are all that remain of the standard motte and bailey castle. Earth was excavated and thrown up to form a small conical earthwork or motte, surrounded by a ditch. On the motte was constructed a wooden palisade within which

The obelisk stands on the motte of the old Norman castle.

CASTLE HOWE 2005 K4702k (Trevor Hughes)

were some form of living quarters. Below the motte the flat area was the traditional bailey on which were housed those who served the castle. On Speed's 1614 map, near the castle is an area named Battyll Place. No evidence has yet come to light about any battle or skirmish there, although human bones have been discovered and both dogs and young children have been known to become slightly disturbed while walking there. This may have something to do with one or other of the Scottish raids of the 12th or 13th centuries, or may only be imagination.

Following the accession of William II (Rufus), a close friend of his, Ivo de Tailebois, presented to the new Benedictine abbey of St Mary in York 'The Church of Kircabi in Kendale with its land.' On the north side of the church was a house which belonged to the abbey and was used by the abbot as his residence when he visited Kendal and was known then as the Abbot's Hall. The present Abbot Hall is an 18th century replacement.

Ivo de Tailebois ruled over Kendal until about the year 1100 when he was succeeded by his son Eldred, or Ethelred, to be followed by

ABBOT HALL 2005 K4703k (Trevor Hughes)

Abbot Hall is now a renowned art gallery.

his son Ketel, whose name is remembered in the parish name of Strickland Ketel. In turn, his son William, the fourth baron of Kendal, changed the family name from its French aspect, causing himself before the king in Parliament to be called William de Lancaster, which title was carried by successive barons until 1240. The second William de Lancaster died in 1184 leaving only a daughter, Helwise, who married Gilbert Fitzrenfred, the baron probably responsible for building Kendal's second castle on the east side of the river. What happened to Castle Howe and why it disappeared is one of Kendal's many unsolved mysteries. Being of wooden construction it could easily have been dismantled as redundant or have been left abandoned to the weather or to recycling by the thrifty Kendalians. It is possible that it might have been destroyed in the Scots raid of 1210.

The economy and prosperity of the town was growing. The wool trade on which it was to be based was increasing and the

HAWES BRIDGE 1891 28623

Hawes Bridge was always a popular place for picnics and was enjoyed by artists and photographers. A short distance away, in Hawes Trough, the river deepens and an old legend says that evil spirits were cast into its depths. Until recent times young mechanics came from work with soap and towel to wash away the day's grime, perhaps getting rid of a few evil spirits too.

church was responsible for much of this. The market was extending from its churchyard base to one where cattle and other farmers and traders came to conduct business and the ordinary people bought their food and other necessities of life. Market rights enabled the baron to exact fees from those who came to market and this augmented his necessary income. Unfortunately, the abbot of St Mary's, York, still held rights over traders on church land, the largest and richest of the markets. King Richard I was engaged on the very expensive Crusades and looked for ways to raise the money he needed. The baron, Gilbert Fitzrenfred, clutched at the opportunity to gain possession of market fees and for the payment of just 20 marks secured

Did you know?

Blind Beck

The beck rises from the hidden fastnesses of Kendal Fell and so some ascribe the word blind to it. It is more likely that blind derives from the ancient word 'blaen' meaning town end or boundary as it was the frontier between Kirkland and Market Kendal.

from the king the town's first charter, granted in 1189, which authorised the holding of a weekly Saturday market.

A GENERAL VIEW FROM CASTLE HILL 1896 38524

Market Kendal was born and grew up alongside but separate from the old church town of Kirkland on the opposite bank of Blind Beck. A charter of liberties was granted to the burgesses of Kendal which set out the basis for market trading and the market in the town expanded. The road through Kirkland was continued into the new town and named Soutergate, the road from the south. It crossed the old church town boundary of Blind Beck by a narrow packhorse bridge which was widened in a later century and is still there underneath the modern road. Market Kendal was, in many ways, beginning to take precedence over Kirkby Kendal.

At an unknown date between 1183 and 1241 the building of the new stone castle was begun, at the summit of a long, whaleback limestone outcrop in a drumlin field of glacial clay and gravel on the east of the river known, self-evidently, for centuries as Castle Hill. The years following the Norman Conquest were turbulent and the barons of Kendal, in common with their neighbouring aristocratic families, needed to create a show of power over the people of the town and district and of solid defence against potential raiders. From time to time, and particularly in the early 14th century, the Scots were an inherent threat. Despite this there is no good evidence of assault or siege and the castle probably spent its days in its strategic position as a fortified manor house dominating the newly formed borough of Kirkby Kendal and Market Kendal alike, the ownership and residency of the castle passing down from baron to baron. The pathways up to it would have been alive with tradesmen, workmen and others going about their business to the Castle Mill by the river or to the town and, from time to time, official visitors and the baron with his family and retinue would pass, making a colourful display. Despite being on the top of a hill, the deep, steep-sided moat or ditch surrounding the castle may well have been watered; it is wet in places now during parts of the year, although it might have been basically dry. Almost from the start it became a convenient place to dump rubbish and the garderobes, or indoor latrines, emptied directly into it. A bridge of some kind, probably a wooden drawbridge, gave entrance to the castle across the moat through a gatehouse. The bailey inside the curtain walls would have been lined with lean-to sheds and workshops. It still contains the remains of a well and the indication of a chapel. The imposing hall block comprised the living quarters of the baron, his family, retainers, servants and administrators who would all have worked and lived in relative comfort, though not to the standard we now enjoy.

The last of the families to live in the castle was the Parrs, through Sir William del Parr's marriage to Elizabeth de Roos in 1383. It passed through the hands of various descendants during the 15th century, until it came to Sir Thomas Parr who was prominent in the court of King Henry VIII, being the Master of the Wards and Comptroller of the King's Households, a most important office. He was an influential man whose life and livelihood was in London and to whom Kendal was as if in a far-off country.

KENDAL CASTLE 1896 38538

KENDAL CASTLE 1914   67370

He removed his household from Kendal in the year 1483 and from that time onwards none of the Parr family actually lived in the castle which, together with the estates, was looked after by a steward. The castle quickly fell into decay; the deer park connected with it was disparked, the vivary (fishpond), rabbit warren and dovecotes abandoned, and the building systematically dismantled, helped by the plundering of useful building materials by the thrifty Kendalians. William

Camden wrote in 1586 that it was ready to fall down with age; there was little of any value left. It became a ruin of romantic aspect and was eventually bought by the corporation in Queen Victoria's Diamond Jubilee year of 1897 to become a place for public enjoyment, and in the last decade has been archaeologically excavated and partly restored.

One of the results of the expansion of the powers and riches of the barony was

Katherine Parr

**KATHERINE PARR'S SIGNATURE, FROM 'DUCHETIANA' BY
SIR G F DUCKETT, 1874** ZZZ04099

King Henry VIII's Queen Regent and surviving wife was born in 1512; we do not know where, but certainly not in Kendal Castle as is often claimed. An exceptionally bright child, astrologers predicted that she was born to sit on the highest seat of imperial majesty, and she eventually did. She was married four times in all, first to Lord Borough as a young teenager; she was widowed at 16, then married Lord Latimer. Two years later she became a widow again and was left a rich woman. She planned to marry Sir Thomas Seymour but was forestalled by the king who took her as his wife in 1543. She was a pious woman; her hand-written Booke of Devotions is preserved in the town hall. It was not an entirely happy marriage. The king's dissolute life caused his death in 1547 and Katherine was freed to marry Sir Thomas, but her joy was short-lived. He was unfaithful to her and she died in childbirth in 1548, her body being buried in Sudeley Church. Kendal is proud of its association with her and has named a school and a road after her.

the rebuilding, enlargement or replacement of the ancient church, either that of supposed Saxon origin or of a later Norman replacement of which we have no evidence, by a fine stone structure. This took place early in the 13th century; during the Victorian restoration work an arch was discovered bearing the date 1201. It has been said that the old church might have been destroyed or mortally desecrated in the Scots raid of 1210, an event that has passed into folk history as 'Kendal's Saddest Day'. On that occasion the Earl of Fife led his men on a periodic border raid, probably in the main for cattle, but entering the church town for plunder. The record written later in the 16th century said that they 'ransacked buildings and killed at random as the mood pleased them. Caring nothing for the authority of the church they killed without mercy a large number of women and children who had sought sanctuary in the church and churchyard.'

THE PARISH CHURCH 1888 21084

Dedicated to the Holy Trinity, the church is always known just as the parish church and it is doubtful if many Kendalians are aware of its actual title. Trinity College, Cambridge, presented rectors and vicars to serve in the church from the Reformation when Queen Mary gave the advowson to the College. Kendal's growing prosperity was shown in the increase in the size of the building. The three central aisles of the present church were built in 1301; the Bellingham (or Lady), Parr and Strickland Chapels were added in the 16th century together with a number of chantry chapels where priests could pray for the souls of the departed. The outer south aisle of the church came in the 15th century and the inner north aisle was added in the 16th century. By the time of its final enlargement the church gained the distinction of being, at 103 feet, the second widest parish church in the country, only seven feet less than York Minster. Much of the finance for all this construction came from the profits of wool trading and the church could certainly vindicate its sobriquet of a woollen church.

Castle Dairy

CASTLE DAIRY, WILDMAN STREET 1924 75806

Of similar date to the castle, Castle Dairy was built in the 14th century and has the honour of being Kendal's oldest continuously occupied house. The name is probably a corruption of the word dowry; it was probably a dower house and the residence of the castle steward or overseer. It was refurbished in 1564 by Anthony Garnett and the exterior has remained virtually unchanged since except for sympathetic renewal of eroded stonework around the windows. Inside, the house remains mainly as Anthony altered it, except for minor changes to suit present needs, and contains some historical gems including his magnificently carved 16th-century bed, perhaps the oldest of its kind still in existence. The whole house is a 400-year-old time capsule set in a 600-year-old building.

STRAMONGATE BRIDGE 1924 75798

Did you know?

Dovecotes

Doves or pigeons were an important source of fresh meat in earlier days. On the gables of Castle Dairy facing Wildman Street can be seen the entrances to the dovecotes in the roof.

Stramongate Bridge over the river was erected some time before the 14th century, a narrow bridge with very steep approaches on each side which caused many accidents.

By 1794 it had become badly decayed and needed complete rebuilding. However, its basic construction was so strong that only blasting could move it, so it was widened instead by building new sections on each side. These divisions can still be seen under the arches. At the southern end of the town is Nether Bridge. It was mentioned in 1376 as Capus Pontus and was probably of wooden construction, wide enough for only one cart. Because of a vast increase in traffic it was doubled in width in 1772, only to be swept away by severe floods after three weeks and had to be hurriedly rebuilt. It was widened again in 1911 and its three sections too can be seen under the arches, especially when illuminated by the Millennium floodlights.

Although somewhat disguised today by a spacious pavement, some visitors wonder why the roadway in the vicinity of the town hall is extra wide. The reason is not immediately obvious and one has to go back to the beginning of the 16th century to find the answer. In about 1500 a new building was set up there known, predictably, as the New Biggin. It was a substantial structure some 30 yards long and 91 yards broad. The passage on the east side was wide enough for wheeled carriages and carts, but that on the other side could only accommodate pedestrians. The building was made of wood, two stories high, the upper storey projecting over a gallery below. On the west side were some small dwellings and one large room, called Cordwainers Hall, belonging to the cordwainers, the last of the Kendal guilds. Shops in the ground floor were traditionally without glass, wooden shutters being lowered to make counters. The east side housed butchers who slaughtered their beasts outside as required by the laws of the time. One can imagine that this, together with the common filthiness, produced highly insanitary conditions. By the end of the 18th century the whole place had become a serious health hazard and carts were finding great difficulty in passing along the road. Half the building belonged to Lady Andover and the other to Lord Lonsdale, bitter political rivals. She said repeatedly that if he were to set fire to his end she would do the same to hers, so removing the nuisance without cost or difficulty once and for all. Naturally, he would not co-operate. After his death in 1803 the corporation obtained

THE NEW BIGGIN FROM 'THE ANNALS OF KENDAL' BY C NICHOLSON 1861 ZZZ04100

KIRKLAND 2005 K4704k (Trevor Hughes)

and immediately demolished it, leaving the town with an enigmatic wide expanse of road.

Towards the end of the 16th century Kirkland, the church town, had settled into a comfortable existence and Market Kendal was growing in size and importance. It had one long street more or less parallelling the river, formed of Soutergate (now Highgate) and Stricklandgate, with the narrow Finkle Street, the road to Scotland, leading from the middle, eastwards to Stramongate, and All Hallows Lane running off to the west. Burgage plots, strips of land leading mainly off the western side of Soutergate and around the Market Place, were rented out by the baron to his tenants or burgesses, for the most part his family and friends, and these

laid the foundation for the famous Kendal yards. Houses were gradually built, quite without any standard plan. Writing in 1769, Dr Wharton described them: 'Excepting the two principal streets, all the houses seem as if they had been dancing a country dance and were out; there they stand, back to back, corner to corner, some up hill, some down, without intent or meaning.' There has been much change over the years but the many different styles and situations of houses in the town add to its charm. The old feudal system was breaking up. Commerce was prospering with Kendal being a natural centre for the south Cumbrian wool trade. The two fairs granted in 1210 were augmented by one more on the eve, feast and morrow of Holy Trinity, and

Sunday trading, after attending to religious observances, was universally acceptable.

The Christian church was not only concerned with its spiritual activities but carried out a temporal ministry. The Augustinian canons of Conishead Priory set up a leper hospital dedicated to St Leonard, just outside and to the north of the town on the road to Appleby, where hospitality was given to needy wayfarers. It was closed at the Reformation and the lands were sold. The only possible remains are a piece of wall that was found at the present Spital Farm. Religious importance was also indicated by the setting up of wayside crosses, particularly at the entrances to the town, often close to sanctuaries or cross houses where travellers could lay themselves before the mercy of God on leaving to face the dangers of rocky or boggy paths, inclement weather, footpads and highwaymen, and to make their devotions and give thanks on returning to the town safely. It is not surprising that some travellers in the Middle Ages wrote their wills before starting a journey. The crosses have all disappeared over time but are called to mind by names such as Stonecross on the Milnthorpe road and Far Cross Bank at the junction of the Shap and Appleby roads. One other cross was the market cross which stood originally in Stricklandgate opposite the present Market Place. In the early centuries the market area was more extensive, spreading beyond the present surrounding buildings and to the west beyond Stricklandgate. It stood on a massive hexagonal stone base and from it monks, friars or other clergy might

have preached to the crowds as the Quaker George Fox did in 1652. It was a place for collecting market tolls and for making official announcements such as proclaiming new monarchs, the opening of fairs, market fees and announcing penalties. It was also the central millarum from which distances along Kendal's high roads were measured.

NETHER BRIDGE 1914   67381

By the 18th century Stricklandgate had become a busy thoroughfare and the cross was a nuisance, so it was moved in 1765 into the Market Place. It had lost its original purpose and by 1900 only part of the base remained, situated at the corner of the old free library which stood on the site of the present war memorial. When the library was demolished in 1909 the stone was moved again to its present position outside the town hall. Known as the Call Stone, it is still used by the town crier for proclamations of national and civic importance but for the most part it provides a seat for the weary, who do not realise its important place in Kendal's long history.

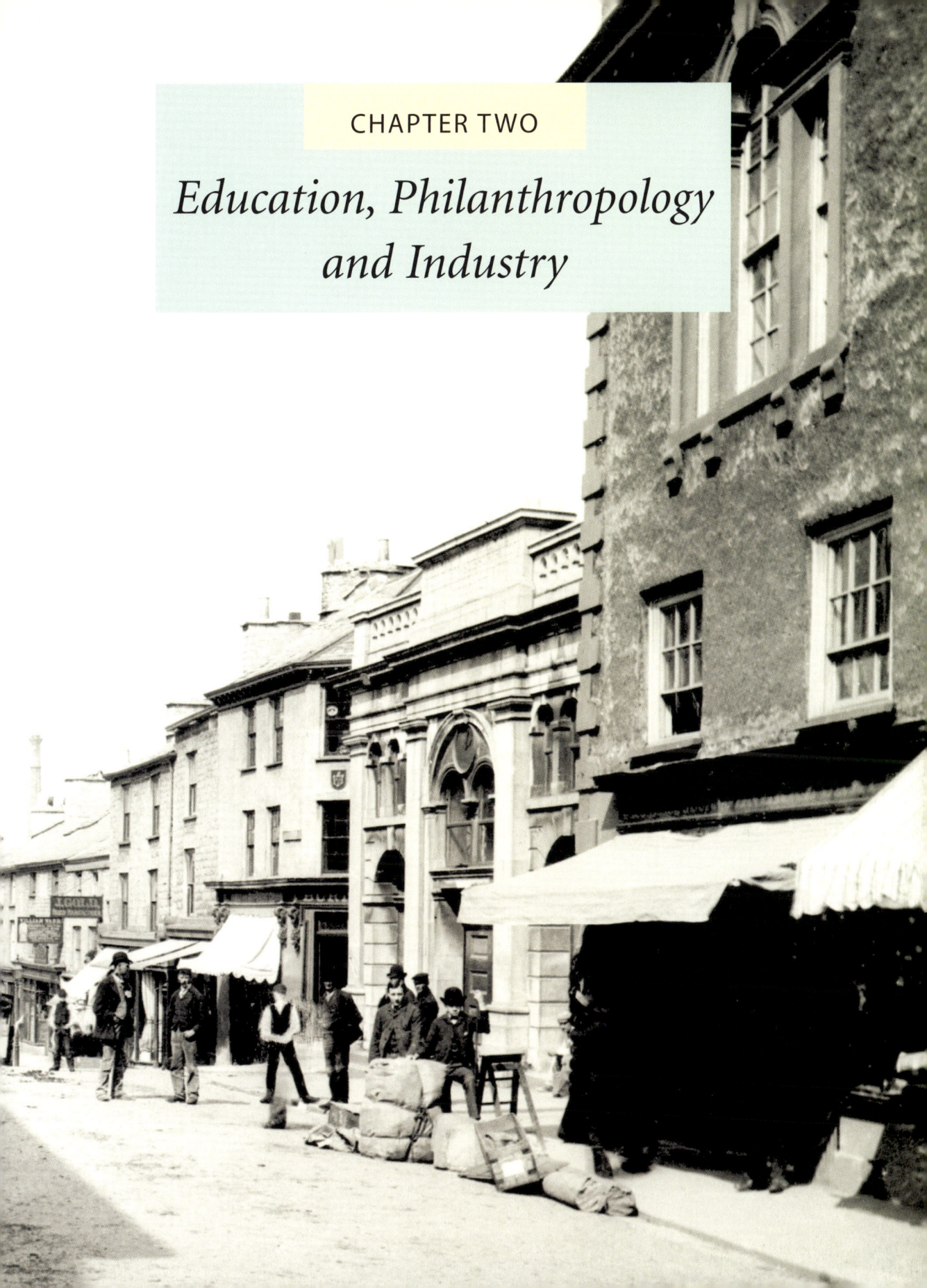

CHAPTER TWO

Education, Philanthropology and Industry

THE YEAR 1575 was a further significant landmark in the development of Kendal. With the Parr family selling their part of the barony, the marquis fee, to the Crown, it became necessary to negotiate new terms for a revision of the Kendal charters of Richard I, Edward II and Edward III so that their authority might be assured. By means of a charter granted by Queen Elizabeth on 28 November 1576, Kendal became a royal borough under the title of 'The Alderman and Burgesses of the Burgh of Kirkby in Kendal', with all its rights and duties deriving directly from the Crown. The old boundaries of Kendal were confirmed and the alderman and burgesses were enjoined to walk them to certify them. The previous baronial, or seignorial, system of government was now superseded, and government was vested in twelve burgesses, one of which was to be elected annually as the chief magistrate and alderman. The corporation was given powers to make and enforce byelaws and was instructed to produce a common seal to ratify and give effect to its decisions.

The first alderman of Kendal was Henry Wilson, a chapman by trade, a general merchant or dealer, whose house, Black Hall, still stands little changed externally in Stricklandgate. Its massive Westmorland chimneys replaced the originals in 1810. The effigy over the front, known as the Bristling Hog, is a renewal of one of the few remaining tradesmen's signs in the town and reminds us that the house became Hodgson's Black Hall Brush Factory in 1838. Black Hall was originally a fine mansion, the home of the Wilson family for many centuries. Henry

THE CORPORATION SEAL OF 1576 FROM 'THE ANNALS OF KENDAL' BY C NICHOLSON 1861
ZZZ04101

Wilson was highly honoured to become the town's first citizen and began well, remaining in post until 1579 when he fell foul of the temptation to which humanity is prone and was stripped of his title, office and burgess-ship on account of his 'living incontinently and having unlawful company with Jennet Eskrige, wife of Christopher Eskrige'. During his time as alderman he presented the corporation with two impressive silver flagons. It appears that the corporation did not find these of much use or value as they exchanged them later for a set of candlesticks, thus negating his memorial. He died and was buried in Kendal parish church on 29 August 1592, so ending a career in public office that bode well but resulted in final ignominy.

In that same year the first moot hall was erected on the south-west corner of the Market Place, a plain building surmounted by a tower. In this hall, acting as a town hall and court, the Council of Burgesses met to conduct corporation business. It was reconstructed in 1759 and gradually fell into

BLACK HALL 2005 K4705k (Trevor Hughes)

disuse and dilapidation. When the courts of session were moved in 1859 to the White Hall, the then new town hall, the building was sold to Job Bintley, the borough surveyor, for £280 and was transformed into a shop. The town clock which used to face Stricklandgate was transferred to St Thomas's Church in 1862 as a gift from the corporation, it being no longer needed to act as general timekeeper for the town. The present building on the site is a replica of the reconstructed hall which was destroyed by arson in 1969.

The new charter gave powers for different timings for the fairs, two of which were now to be held annually, one 'on the eve, day and morrow of the feast of St Mark,' 29 April, and the other 'on the eve, day and morrow of the feast of St Simon and St Jude,' 28 October. The corporation licensed traders, collected market tolls and fines and controlled the quality of cottons (the name for woollen cloths derived from the word coatings) and linens sold in the town, and the weight of bread and other foodstuffs. It also maintained the town jail. The administration of the corporation was set down in great detail in the Boke off Recorde of 1575 which contains the earliest records of the borough. John Speed wrote in his book, 'The Historie of Great Britaine' in 1610, 'Kendal is a place of very civill and orderly government' and so in the main it was. He annotated his map of Westmorland with the words, 'The Countie of Westmorland and Kendall the chief towne described.' He included the first known map of Kendal and, as was his custom, decorated it with a self-designed coat of arms, the quarters of the shield probably depicting bale hooks and teasels, symbols of Kendal's wool trade. There has been dispute as to whether the teasels were in fact meant to be pack needles or spindles but teasels have been commonly accepted. He did not invent the motto, *Pannus mihi panis*, which was added later. It is commonly translated as 'Wool is my bread' although scholars state that as the latin for wool is *Lanus* and not *Pannus* it should properly read 'Cloth is my bread'. In 1629 Thomas Sleddall, the mayor at the time, presented the corporation with a silver tankard engraved with Speed's shield backed by a representation of a leather hide, tanning being another of Kendal's staple industries, together with the motto. This coat of arms, prominent over the entrance to the town hall, eventually became established and replaced the 1575 seal but it was not officially recognised by the College of Heralds until 1993!

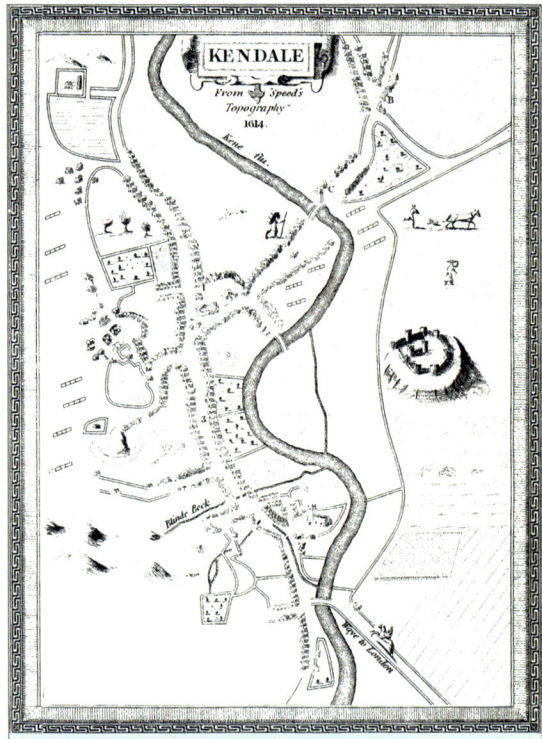

JOHN SPEED'S MAP OF KENDAL IN 1614 FROM 'THE ANNALS OF KENDAL' BY C NICHOLSON 1861
ZZZ04102

Did you know?

Tenters

After dyeing and fulling, woollen cloth was washed and hung on tenter frames to dry and stretch. The frames had a series of oak pegs or metal hooks to hold the cloth to keep its width constant. Tenters were erected in ranks on terraces in many places in Kendal. The road High Tenterfell preserves the name.

THE KING'S ARMS HOTEL 1924 75800

The King's Arms Hotel was one of Kendal's most famous coaching inns and was reputed to serve the best hot food in the town.

A KING'S ARMS HOTEL ADVERTISEMENT FROM A LOCAL GUIDE BOOK OF 1926
ZZZ04103 (Trevor Hughes Collection)

Kendal continued to develop as a market town with its quite separately administered neighbouring church township of Kirkland. William Camden described it at the end of the 16th century as having one of the best corn markets in the northern parts. The town was reaching a high point in its evolution. It was noted by Celia Fiennes in 1682 as a good trading town and by the Rev Thomas Machell in 1697 as a most famous town for its industry. Daniel Defoe, in 1700, called it a rich and populous town, and Sir Daniel Fleming of Rydal wrote in 1671, 'It is a great market and the chief town for largeness, neatness, buildings and trade in this county. …….. This town is seated in very good air, and its healthfulness is improved partly by the cleanliness of the people, and partly by its situation on a hillside, the river carrying away whatever filthiness the descending rain washes out of it.' Of course, such descriptions are relative to the accepted standards of the time; the river acted as a drain or sewer from the streets and houses, the noisome trades and industries and the increasing number of mills along its banks.

A feature of Kendal's business life was the organisation of the various trades into guilds, an early form of trade union or protection society. These harked back to medieval times but the early records of them can no longer be found. There were twelve companies or guilds covering the various trades and professions, grouped in similar kinds of occupation such as chapmen (agents and pedlars), merchants and [dry] salters (general traders), and, indicating a descending rank of respectability, innkeepers, alehousekeepers and tiplers (beerhousekeepers). Among trades which have disappeared were the armourers, bowyers,

STRAMONGATE, YARD 65 1914
67386

Typical of Kendal's old yards where the ground floors were often used as workshops, this was demolished for redevelopment. One of the cottages has a long-case window.

Black Drop

Black Drop was one of those universal remedies for all ills common throughout the centuries. Margaret Braithwaite sold 'The Genuine Quaker Black Drop' in Kirkland in 1822. It was made of opium, quince juice, saffron, cloves, nutmeg and cinnamon, simmered for four weeks. The compound was expensive, selling at ten shillings for a four-ounce phial plus one shilling government tax, and was popular all over Westmorland and North Lancashire. It was made by others who all proclaimed that theirs was the best, like Hannah Backhouse of Stramongate who, in her advertisements, claimed to be the sole possessor of the recipe of 'The Original Black Drop', and Ann Todd, who died in 1820 at the age of 72, maintaining that she alone had the true recipe. The Westmorland Gazette cynically said it 'seemed to vie with wool as the staple commodity of Kendal.' The active ingredient was opium which was taken almost universally then against pain and discomfort and for recreational purposes. Thomas de Quincy, 'The Opium Eater', was a notable example in Kendal, and the poet Samuel Taylor Coleridge fell foul of the addictive nature of the drug and was determined to warn others of the danger of its continued use.

fletchers and spurriers who produced armour, longbows, arrows and spurs respectively. These trades take us back into an early form of warfare, to the Battle of Halidon Hill in 1333 where the superiority of the English longbow was first demonstrated, and to the Battle of Flodden Field of 1513 where the famous Kendal bowmen displayed their prowess, immortalised by Sir Walter Scott in his poem about the battle, and by Shakespeare describing the skirmish on Godshill in his play, 'Henry IV, Part 1'. Some trades such as the websters (weavers) and skinners (furriers) are still remembered in common surnames today.

The Boke off Recorde set out clearly the duties, responsibilities and powers of the guilds. Each craft was only allowed to engage in its own type of work – an early form of closed shop. Failure to obtain membership of the appropriate guild meant virtual exclusion from legitimate trading. Once in about every 21 years the guilds in Kendal held a procession through the town, each guild with its decorated waggons carrying splendid displays, depicting its craft and wares or classical scenes or men in fancy dress, accompanied by contingents of marching men carrying the tools of their trade. Each guild had its own distinctive colours and emblems and endeavoured to eclipse all others in extravagant magnificence. As the years passed, the high cost of mounting processions was such that many a trader faced financial ruin and 1759 saw the last of them; it was probably the grandest of all. Over 1,000 took part, led by more than six hundred men engaged in the woollen trades with the mayor, aldermen and gentlemen bringing up the rear. The cheers of the crowds and sounds of the bands all combined to make a merry cacophony. After this great day the

Window Tax

The window tax was imposed in 1697, on the number of windows in each house having more than six windows and worth more than £5 per annum, the tax being enacted to pay for the recoinage of silver. To avoid the tax, windows were blocked up or one long narrow window was made to serve more than one floor. Westmorland long-case windows can be seen in older houses in Kendal. This one in Stramongate is 33 feet tall but only 2 feet 9 inches wide.

A WESTMORLAND LONG-CASE WINDOW
2005 K4706k (Trevor Hughes)

power and influence of the guilds declined with the growth of population, the fastest in the town's history then or since, and it became more difficult to register and control the increasing numbers of strangers (non-guild members), foreigners (from out of the town) and freemen, leaving the cordwainers to become the last of the Kendal guilds to operate. They closed their doors in 1799, on account of being unable to win their case of imposing a fine of £10 on a stranger who attempted to do business in the town.

The earliest school in Kendal was the free school, founded in 1525 by Adam Penyngton of Boston, Lincolnshire. It was a chantry school, the boys being taught in the parish church. After the Reformation it was sold off by the Crown and in 1588 Miles Philipson of Crook gave a parcel of the Abbot Hall land with a house for a new free school 'for the godly and virtuous education, instruction and institution of youth of the town and parish of Kendal, in grammar and other good learning.' The school was built by public subscription in money and kind and replaced the earlier school as a Grammar School. In

1641 the Moot Hall Court ordained that no child was to be admitted to or be taught in the school who was unable to read the psalter or who could only read from the Horn Book ABC and Primer lest they hindered the progress of the majority. The school had its ups and downs and at one time was almost faced with closure but it survived, moving in 1889 to its present site on the edge of the town. The old school buildings were converted into a cottage and later became part of today's Museum of Lakeland Life and Industry.

The school was not the only essay into education in the town. In 1670 the philanthropist Thomas Sandes established a hospital or almshouses in Highgate for eight poor widows where he employed a schoolmaster to read prayers to them daily and to teach poor boys until they were ready to attend the Grammar School. He also set up a trust to pay £5 a year for seven years for a poor boy to be sent from the Grammar School to Queen's College free of charge with an additional £1 a year to be given to the boy for his expenses. He insisted that the boy, chosen by the mayor and corporation, should not be a 'richman's son'. The gatehouse of Sandes Hospital served as a schoolroom and library, and the work of the schoolmaster led to the formation of the Bluecoat School in a tall building at the head

THE GATEHOUSE OF SANDES HOSPITAL, HIGHGATE 1914 67385

of the almshouse gardens which, together with the gatehouse and almshouses, can still be seen. Only boys were taught at first since only boys went to the Grammar School but in 1714 girls were admitted and were taught by Isobel Fisher. From that year the scholars were all dressed in a blue uniform. The school prospered and in 1886 merged with the new Grammar School.

SANDES HOSPITAL ALMSHOUSES 1914 67399

The pointed windows at the far end are in the Bluecoat School which was endowed by Thomas Sandes.

The Friends' School, primarily for children of Quaker families, opened in 1698 beside the Meeting House in Stramongate, being added to by a boarding establishment in 1728 and all moving in 1772 to a new building on the opposite side of the road. The famous scientist John Dalton was a master there between 1785 and 1793 and is said to have been rather too keen on using the cane. This school also prospered, with changes, into the modern era.

A new charter was granted by Charles I in 1637, a lengthy document confirming the rights granted under the Elizabethan charter and adding further privileges, one of which was permission to use the title of mayor in place of chief magistrate, the leading citizen. Thomas Sleddall was the first to carry this title. A sword bearer, two sergeants at mace and a clerk of the market were appointed and a searcher of cottons was empowered to test the quality of woollen goods produced and sold in the town. Hawkers and pedlars were allowed only to sell their goods in the open market or at fairs, the borough being given powers to control all markets, fairs, courts leet and pie powder. Powers were granted to commit felons, malefactors and disturbers of the peace to the prison, or town jail, known as the Court Loft. This, with its dungeon called the Black Hole, was situated below the market hall close to the moot hall in the

THE MARKET 1924 75795

Market Place. This charter lasted for only some 15 years, passing through the turbulent Cromwellian period. With the restoration of the monarchy and Charles II on the throne, his Chief Justice, the notorious Judge Jeffries, who annulled many town charters, 'persuaded' the corporation to dispense with its charter too. Left with no official rights and privileges the town had to beg a new charter from Charles II which was granted in 1681, and was received in the town amidst scenes of great celebration. It turned out to be somewhat of a disappointment as it failed to include any of the concessions asked for, such as the cancellation of the yearly rent to the Crown for the market tolls; in fact the rent was increased. Powers to impose tolls on raw hides and apples, which were previously exempt, and tolls applied on goods crossing the two bridges in the town were not even mentioned. The first mayor appointed by the new charter was Lancelot Forth of whom we know nothing except that he was a pewterer. There was something of a snub in the clause which reserved to the Crown the right to displace the mayor, aldermen or any other officers at its pleasure. For good or ill, the charter stood, demonstrating the power of the monarch over the corporation, and remained the basis of local government for some two hundred years until 1835. The Elizabethan and the two Caroline charters are stored in the town hall but are not on public view.

It was another royal Charles who brought excitement and apprehension to the town in 1745 when Bonnie Prince Charlie, the Young Pretender to the English throne, came

PRINCE CHARLIE'S HOUSE 2005 K4707k (Trevor Hughes)

into the town with his army, pausing to hear his father being proclaimed as King James III from the market cross and receiving assurance from the mayor that the people of Kendal, who were terrified, would give no trouble. The Scottish rebels were in high spirits and marched cheerfully on south to London. Three weeks later the atmosphere had changed for the worse as the demoralised tatters of the army on its retreat from defeat at Derby came again into the town. It was market day and, so the story goes, the mayor on his white horse, seeing his advantage, ordered the stallholders to meet the rebels with a fusillade of fruit, vegetables and anything else at hand.

A skirmish broke out and the mayor managed to escape to safety. The rebels moved off into the enclosed space by the fish market behind the Pump Inn at the head of Finkle Street and, feeling trapped, fought their way down the street where during the affray one of them was shot. A purse, possibly his, was found when clearing up and is preserved in Kendal museum. A farmer from nearby New Hutton, John Slack, was also killed in the crossfire. A legend recounts that some of the rebel soldiers rushed into the Angel Inn in Highgate from which the family fled for their lives leaving in their panic a young child standing in a passage. Beside her was seen an angel holding a drawn sword. The soldiers interpreted this as a sign that God was protecting her so, with superstitious fear, they turned tail and left, giving rise to a possible origin for the name of the Inn. Meanwhile, while all this was going on, the Prince was enjoying the hospitality of Justice Thomas Shepherd in his house at the northern end of Stricklandgate, still known today as 'Prince Charlie's House', where he slept the night in comfort. He was furious when he heard the news of the shooting of one of his men and fined the town for the outrage. However, there was no time to be lost as his pursuer, the Duke of Cumberland, 'The Butcher,' was in hot pursuit so the Prince and the remnant of his army left the town with alacrity. Ironically, the duke also rested in the same house and even slept the night in the same bed! The duke's name is immortalised in that of a public house on the junction of the two roads at Far Cross Bank.

SIZERGH CASTLE 1896 38542

Sizergh Hall was built in the 14th century and a pele tower and great hall were added to form a fortified mansion, now called the castle. It has been in the hands of the Strickland family for over 700 years. Katherine Parr was related to Lady Strickland and it is claimed that she slept in the hall.

This whole era was a troublous time. During the earlier Civil War between King and Parliament, loyalties in Kendal fluctuated from one cause to the other – Parliamentary to Royalist and back again – though it is likely that the ordinary townsfolk would have been in the main indifferent until the Royalists under Sir Marmaduke Langdale passed through pursued by the Parliamentarians, led by Lord Fairfax, who harried the town. For more than half a year the troops of both sides, joined by the Scots, fought around Kendal. The Parliamenterians under the Kendalian Colonel Briggs chased the Royalists north into the Lake District and besieged the Royalist,

Robert Philipson of Crook, in his home at Belle Isle on Windermere. After ten days Briggs was called to take his forces to Carlisle which he did on a Sunday, by way of Kendal. He attended the service in the parish church, taking the opportunity to monitor how well or not the service was being conducted on the prescribed lines, while Robert's brother Huddleston relieved him to ride after Briggs and take revenge. Robert, nicknamed Robert the Devil, with a small contingent of troops, found Briggs in the church and rode, following him down one aisle and up the other, striking his head on leaving the west door and losing his helmet. Briggs escaped and Robert, having killed one of his men, galloped back to Belle Isle. An old helmet, called 'The Rebel's Cap,' and a sword are hung up today high above the left-hand aisle. It is unlikely that they were actually Robert's but are a constant reminder of unsettled times when religion and warfare were intertwined.

Religion played a crucial part in the development of the town in the late 17th century when George Fox brought the Society of Friends, or Quakers, to Kendal, countering the current religious lassitude and apathy. He is known to have preached from the market cross in 1652. Early adherents suffered loss

PARISH CHURCH 1914   67374

of property, family and reputation and were maligned as 'delinquents and papists' but persevered in their faith; under the terms of the Declaration of Indulgence of 1687 under King James II they were included in those who were henceforth enabled to worship and work to some extent unhindered. The Kendal

Quaker Meeting built a meeting house in Stramongate for its base, and during the following century Quakers grew in prosperity, power and influence in the town, so much so that Kendal became virtually a Quaker town for some two hundred years. Notable among Quaker business men were the Wakefields and the Crewdsons who opened the first two banks in the town on the same day, 1 January 1788. The Wakefield Bank first traded from John Wakefield's house in Stricklandgate and moved in 1799 to a site now covered by the modern Elephant Yard shopping mall. The bank of Maude, Wilson and Crewdson was sited first in Stramongate, moving in its turn to Highgate in 1792, becoming Crewdson's Bank in 1803. The two banks amalgamated in 1840 as The Kendal Bank and relocated later to the present site where the building, now Barclays Bank, still bears the old name incised on its frontage. True to their religious principles, the Quaker banks were seen from the beginning to be honest, trustworthy and reliable. In 1797, during the Napoleonic Wars, the Bank of England lost its ability to pay in gold coinage and sacrificed the trust of the people. The Kendal Bank issued its own banknotes and, almost alone during times of national financial crisis, held its head high, its reputation being recognised within and outside Kendal. The Bank of Westmorland, designed by the Kendal architect George Webster, was built in 1834. It too prospered and was trusted, carrying above its portico a lion couchant, indicating financial strength. The lion is made of Coade stone, an artificial stone popular in the early 19th century.

THE KENDAL BANK 2005 K4708k (Trevor Hughes)

KENDAL
BANKS.

WE, the Undersigned Inhabitants of the Town of Kendal, having the most perfect confidence in the Stability of the Bank of Messrs. WILSON, CREWDSON & CO., and also in that of Messrs. J. WAKEFIELD & SONS, in consequence of the opulence and prudence of the Partners in the said Firms, do voluntarily pledge ourselves not only to take their Notes in Payment, but also that we are willing to guarantee Money lodged in either of the said Banks to any Amount. As witness our hands this 13th Day of February, 1826.

GEO. FORREST, MAYOR.	J. HUDSON, VICAR	T. H. MAUDE, Esq.
JOHN PEARSON	ANTHONY YEATES	JAMES GANDY & SONS
THOS. COOKSON & SON	GEORGE YEATES	I. & W. WILSON
JOS. BRAITHWAITE	A. SHEPHERD, Shaw End	ISAAC WHITWELL
ROBERT BENSON	JOHN NEWBY	DANIEL HARRISON
JOS. & JNO. ATKINSON	R. GREENHOW & Co.	WILLIAM GELDARD
THOMAS REVELEY	SMITH WILSON,	I. WILSON, SOLICITOR
JAS. SINKINSON	SIMPSON & IRELAND	JOHN GASKARTH
M. & R. BRANTHWAITE	T. WILSON & SONS	JONATHAN HODGSON
ISAAC RIGGE	JOHN IRELAND	J. IRELAND & Co.
FRANCIS WEBSTER	G. & M. GIBSON	RICHARD RAWES
ZEPHANIAH BANKS	THOMAS GREENHOW	
THOS. HARRISON, SUR.	E. TATHAM, SOLICITOR	

Printed by Tyras Redhead, Gazette-Office, Kendal.

KENDAL BANKS POSTER
ZZZ04104 (Trevor Hughes Collection)

Confidence was expressed in the Kendal banks at a time of national financial depression.

Did you know?

Savings Bank

Priscilla Bell of the Wakefield banking family founded the first savings bank in 1798, a benefit club for women. The Kendal branch opened in 1816 and by 1860 there were no less than three thousand depositors. When it was wound up in 1890 it gave five thousand pounds towards the corporation's purchase of the Kendal Castle grounds and Abbot Hall Park.

It was not only the Quakers who revived Christian worship and service in Kendal. John Wesley too despaired of the parlous state of the established church and, after a moment of enlightenment in London, travelled about the country on horseback preaching as he went to turn people back to a strong, devout faith. He visited Kendal a number of times, and on the first occasion in 1753 was disgusted by the attitude of the people who came to hear him preach by coming in late and sitting down without preparing themselves by prayer. However they were obviously impressed by his preaching, as some of them followed him to the inn where he was staying and urged him to preach to them again. It was one of Wesley's colleagues, John Whitefield, who really led the way in Kendal, the work being

THE WESLEYAN CHAPEL 1888   21090

carried on by Stephen Brunskill. He preached hell-fire sermons, at least once from the steps of the old theatre in the Market Place, which was then being used as a place of worship and now bears the words 'Working Men's Institute', indicating its later use. A purpose-built chapel was erected in 1808 at the foot of House of Correction Hill, which soon greatly outgrew its congregation and was rebuilt in 1883 in the form of the present church.

John Wesley was unenamoured with the general state and dangers of the Cumbrian roads, and welcomed the improvements that came with the turnpikes. For a very long time the local parishes were responsible for the upkeep of their roads but repair and maintenance often left much to be desired,

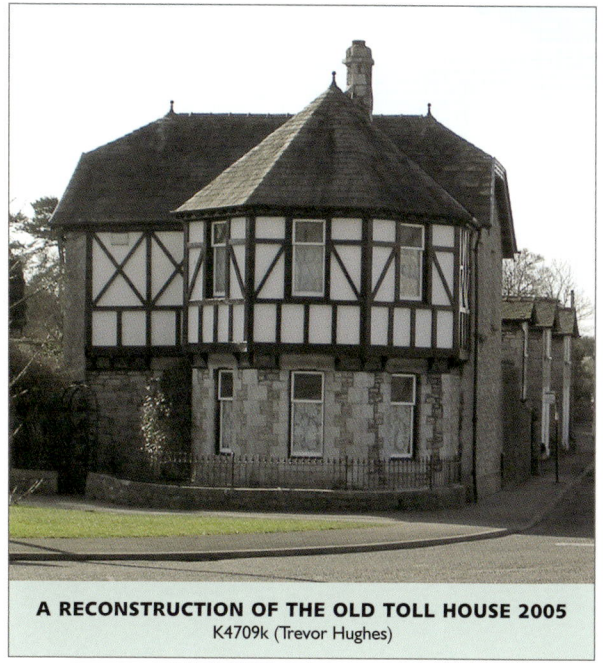

A RECONSTRUCTION OF THE OLD TOLL HOUSE 2005
K4709k (Trevor Hughes)

George Romney

THE PARISH CHURCH FONT 1924 75812

THE MEMORIAL TO GEORGE ROMNEY
ZZZ04105 (Trevor Hughes)

The memorial to the artist George Romney is on the left.

Lest Kendal be thought of as only a place of trade and industry, it is well to remember its artistic and literary merits. At the entrance to the town from Milnthorpe in the south stands Romney House where, at some time lived George Romney, a famous portrait painter. Born in Dalton-in-Furness, he developed a passion for the arts and was apprenticed in Kendal to a portrait painter, Christopher Steele. In time he set up on his own and scratched a meagre living until in his twenties he raised fifty pounds and moved to London where he began to achieve success. He travelled the continent improving his style and became accepted as a talented artist. One of his important commissions was to paint the Gower family, a painting which is held in the Abbot Hall art gallery in the town. He also made violins and played one in his studio to gain inspiration for his paintings. He eventually became senile and, his health fading fast, he died in the care of his faithful and long-suffering wife, helpless as a baby, in 1802.

especially with the introduction of wheeled carts, wagons and carriages. Towards the end of the 17th century turnpike trusts were set up to levy tolls on road users. Kendal had no less than nine major roads converging on it. Fore-runner of the modern A6 road was the Heronsyke to Eamont Bridge turnpike running from the Lancashire border, over Shap to that of Cumberland. To the south of Kendal the turnpike ran via the village of Natland to Keighley, then part of the main road to London and extensively used for commercial traffic. The Nether Bridge toll was set up near the foot of the bridge where the modern reconstruction of the toll house now stands. Another toll bar was situated to the north of the town at Plumgarths on the Windermere road; modern road improvements have obliterated all traces. People tried in every way to avoid passing through the toll bar and using the turnpike, and this led to the decline of the trusts whose responsibilities were eventually taken over by local authorities.

John Gough was born in Stramongate in 1757 and at the age of only six was made almost completely blind by an attack of smallpox. He was a boy of intense curiosity, a talent which held him in good stead in his later years when, despite his handicap, he became so proficient in Latin, natural philosophy and mathematics that he was able to teach a number of eminent scholars, including John Dalton. He wrote many learned articles, essays and treatises and became famous as 'The Blind Philosopher.' Repeated attacks of epilepsy led to his death in 1825.

Tribute must also be paid to Bernard Gilpin,

> # *Did you know?*
>
> ## *Chambers' Encyclopaedia*
>
> *Ephraim Chambers was a pupil at the old grammar school in Kendal. He became concerned that so much knowledge was scattered among hundreds of volumes, so he compiled the world's first encyclopaedia. First published in 1728 as 'The Dictionary of Arts and Sciences', it occupied the rest of his life and has gone through countless editions right into the present day. He died in 1749 and was buried in Westminster Abbey.*

who was given the epithet 'The Apostle of the North.' He was born in Kentmere Hall, just outside the town, in 1517, and became provost of Queen's College, Oxford. He was a zealous Protestant evangelist and toured the north of England preaching, refusing the Bishopric of Carlisle. He had no time for nominal Christianity and on entering the pulpit in the parish church on one occasion he castigated the church officers and the congregation in the strongest terms for their sacrilege in allowing a person to hang up a glove in a prominent place in the church as a threat to fight to resolve a quarrel. He was also keen on education and was one of the donors to the subscription for founding the second free Grammar School that was set up beside the church.

LEVENS HALL c1900   K4504t

Levens Hall was built as a pele tower and hall in the 14th century and was transformed into an Elizabethan mansion in 1489, containing fine furniture, oak panelling and plasterwork. The gardens are famous for their topiary.

The Kendal Fell Trust was formed in 1767 with the aim and duty to help the poor and to assist the town with its lighting and street cleaning, using income from rent and rates imposed on those using Kendal Fell, an enclosed tract of common land north-west of the town. The Trust established the town poor house in 1769, where men and women were housed and worked separately as was the case generally in similar institutions, and there was a schoolroom for boys. The inmates had to earn their keep, the men being employed in work such as breaking stones for the roads and the women in spinning, carding, weaving and knitting. A fever ward was later converted into a girls' schoolroom and a garden was cultivated by the inmates to supplement the food provided. The diet was basic and unadventurous and the beds were searched each morning for fleas. In its later years a house of recovery, or hospital, was added and it was taken over as a workhouse by the Poor Law Union in 1836. Having long outlived its purpose the workhouse became a geriatric hospital, closing in the 1990s, the site now being covered by housing.

Higher up the hill above the workhouse a house of correction was built in the late 16th century, a euphemism for a prison. It consisted of one small room for both men and women, having one tiny window, no chimney, no courtyard, no water and no sewer. The keeper and his family lived together with the prisoners and were provided with a garden. The building was ill-built with a thatched roof, hardly rating as secure, though there were never more than one or two prisoners to accommodate and the regime was somewhat lax. The keeper, Miles Hayton, is known to have been in the habit of taking prisoners for a walk on fine afternoons to play football on Tenter Fell, warning them to follow him when he returned saying that if they didn't he would lock them out! He received his just deserts when a woman prisoner, Mol Ward, escaped from his custody in London where he had taken her to be transported. Isabel Lewis was arrested in Kirkland in 1776 for stealing a cloak worth ten pennies from Anne Garnett and was imprisoned. Two of her friends, Miles Wilson and Daniel Tomlinson, broke a large hole in the prison wall and set her free; she was never recaptured. Over the door of the prison was a stone slab bearing the words, 'If people woulde be goode and live in feare the Justices woulde never send them here.' A scold's bridle, used to silence nagging women, reputedly recovered from the prison, is held in Kendal museum.

A new stone prison replaced the old one in 1786, surrounded by a wall some 40 feet high in places. This, also known as the house of correction, was in complete contrast to the old prison being as clean and comfortable as a prison ever can be. As in the workhouse, men and women were kept separate. Elizabeth Fry, the prison reformer, visited the new prison a year after it had been virtually rebuilt in 1817 and was suitably impressed. Beggars and vagabonds as well as thieves and other felons were sent to the house of correction, sometimes having been paraded through the streets half-naked or having been whipped first with the cat o' nine tails. Margaret

Fuller's punishment for stealing peats was to be carried in a cart from the house of correction to Blind Beck Bridge in the middle of January, naked from the waist upwards, and with the word 'Thief' written in large letters on her torso. It was decreed that she was then to be discharged – if she had not already died of cold on the way! With its high walls and heavy bolted doors the place was secure but, nevertheless, escapes were made. Under the Prisons Act of 1877 the house of correction's title was changed to Kendal prison and in 1888 it became the county gaol when that at Appleby closed. It became less used over the years and closed as a civil prison in 1894, remaining in use for military prisoners until the end of the Boer War in 1901. Six years later the building was bought at auction for £1,000 by W F Pennington who used it as a source of building material, taking some 20 years to complete the demolition. Just a small section of the exterior wall still rises above the roadway to show where the prison was.

1688 was the momentous year when the Stuart King James II misguidedly tried to impose Catholicism on the country. Most of the country rose up against him and a convention of Whigs and Tories in London invited William of Orange to invade England and overthrow James. This he did in 1688 and James fled to France leaving the throne vacant, William and Mary occupying it when crowned the following year. By this 'Glorious Revolution', Catholicism was cast out in favour of Protestantism, and the Toleration Act of 1689 granted freedom of worship to Protestant dissenters, an important consequence for Kendal, although municipal offices were still denied them. In the century that followed England was ruled by the Hanoverian Georges, none of whom gained universal public approbation. George III attacked the Whig aristocrats' ruling oligarchy to claim back the royal prerogative and this angered them intensely. The Whigs of the Kendal Fell Trust so vehemently disliked the Georgian monarch that in 1788, the centenary of the Glorious Revolution, they erected a monument on the mound of Castle Howe. To this day the monument bears a plaque in memory of the Revolution, containing the words 'Sacred to Liberty', shades of the clarion call of the French Revolution of the following year, 'Liberty, Equality, Fraternity', although politically neither the Whigs nor the opposing Tories would have agreed with equality between them. The original plaque, broken in two, is preserved in Kendal museum.

Did you know?
The Elba Monument
In opposition to the Whigs' monument on Castle Howe the Tory, James Bateman of Tolson Hall, had an obelisk constructed in a field near the present Plumgarths roundabout on the Windermere road, celebrating the defeat of Napoleon in 1814, only to be frustrated by his escape from Elba to continue the war. The monument now stands, with a plaque but no purpose.

COUNTY MAP OF WESTMORLAND SHOWING KENDAL c1850

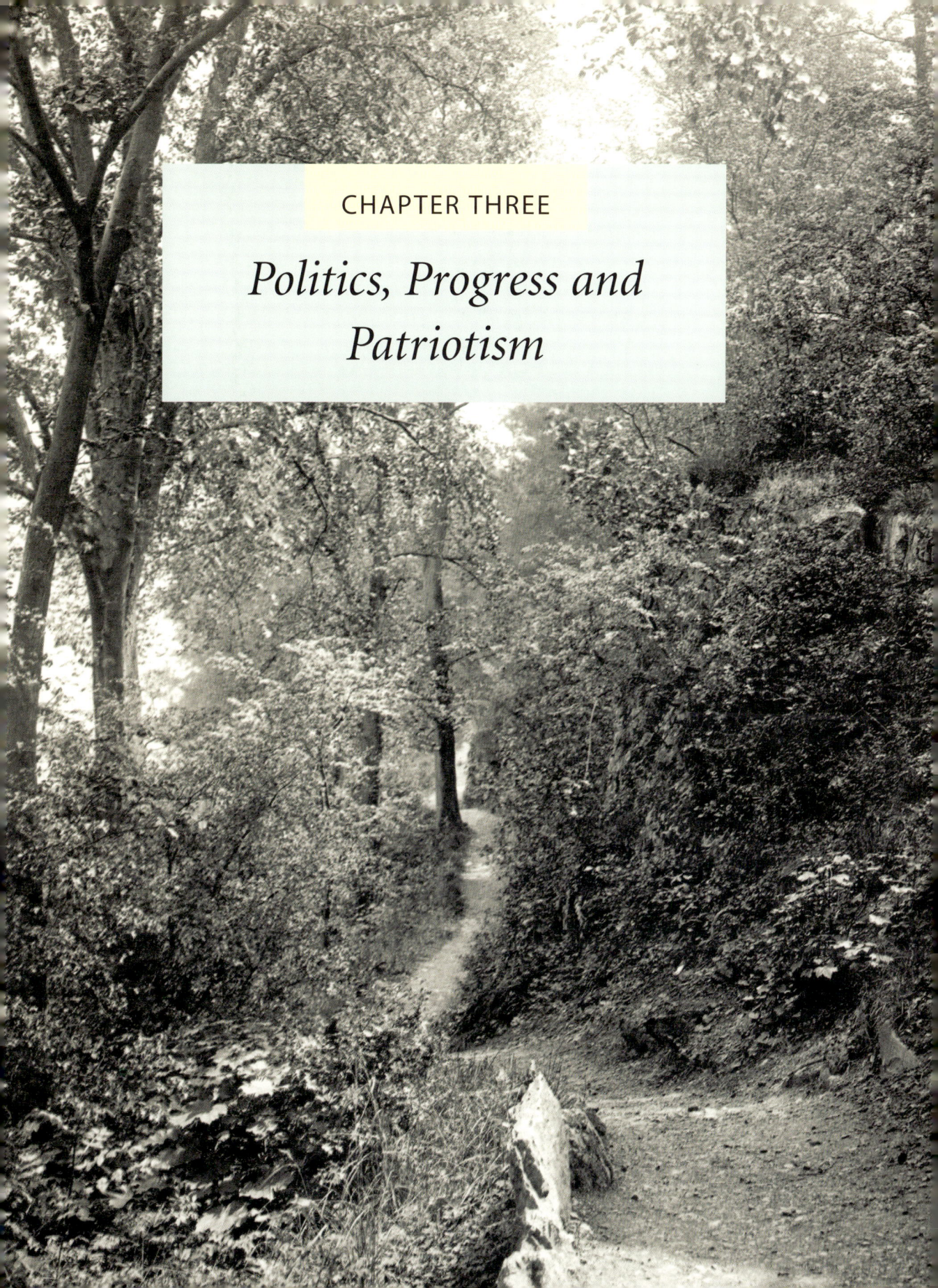

CHAPTER THREE

Politics, Progress and Patriotism

THE 19TH CENTURY began in an atmosphere of political rivalry between the two parties, the Whigs and the Tories, which developed into the Liberals and Conservatives respectively. Leading the Whigs in Kendal was Henry Brougham, his party colour being blue, Lord and Colonel Lowther being the Tory champions with their colour of yellow. The Parliamentary elections in 1818 saw the town split between the two factions with the newly founded Westmorland Gazette favouring the Tories, The Westmorland Advertiser and Kendal Chronicle backing the Whigs. The arrival of the Lowthers and Brougham into the town to announce their standing for election sparked off riots, both sides being

STRICKLANDGATE 1914   67369

equally guilty in bribing potential voters with lavish dinners, copious draughts of ale and the like. Despite Brougham's pious hope that his supporters would behave with dignity, when the Lowther party marched in procession round the town with their yellow banner and ribbons flying, trouble was inevitable. As they passed

the Commercial Inn in Stricklandgate a howling mob broke all its windows and the cavalcade was pelted with missiles and garbage. Rioters attacked the King's Arms Hotel and invaded the White Hart, causing considerable damage there too. Honour was restored when Brougham's blue banner was torn down in retaliation.

Things were no better in the elections of 1820. The newspapers were clearly partisan in their reporting, The Kendal Chronicle stating blandly that 'Mr Henry Brougham entered the town escorted by a numerous gathering of the friends of independence, accompanied by music playing and colours flying.' In contrast, The Westmorland Gazette took a jaundiced view of the same event saying that, 'Disconsolate Mr Brougham, arriving in a shabby gig, was met and accompanied by a rabble, chiefly women and children of the most beggarly description, engaged for the purpose. Mr Brougham was so much ashamed of his followers that he gave them the slip and entered the Fox and Goose from a window of which he made a speech, accompanied by a man with a black eye.' The Lowthers won the election and on the occasion of the voting the military were called out in readiness, soon quelling the minor rioting that took place. The Lowthers were heartily disliked by sections of the population of the town, so much so that when the street was opened beside the town hall down to the river, they refused to acknowledge the official name of Lowther Street and would only refer to it as 'the new street'.

To be Sold by Private Contract,

NINE Freehold DWELLING-HOUSES; each House making a Vote; situate on the House of Correction Hill, Kendal.

For further Particulars apply to James Martindale, the owner, on the Premises.

N. B. None need apply but *Blues.*

Kendal, Jan. 5, 1819.

BLUE BUILDINGS NOTICE ZZZ04106 (Trevor Hughes Collection)

OLD POLICE OFFICE YARD 1914 67388

One of the results of the political opposition was the construction of a small grid of streets in the northern end of the town at the foot of House of Correction Hill where the Kendal Union Building Society, established in 1818, built houses. The shares of the Society were taken up by the Whig, or Blue, Party with the purpose of obtaining votes for Henry Brougham. The prospective owners of each house, who would have the 40 shillings freehold that allowed them the right to vote, were required to show that they were true blue supporters, opposed to the hated Lowther Toryism. The houses became known as The Blue Buildings and one of the streets was named Caroline Street after the wife of King George IV who, with Tory government support, the king was attempting to divorce. When the queen arrived in England church bells were rung in Kendal and some homes, probably those of Whig supporters, were illuminated.

The Municipal Corporations Act of 1835 had a significant effect on local government in the town. It modified the authority of the charters and gave the right to vote to elect councillors to all male property owners. It opened the door to a number of important improvements such as the foundation of the paid police force, consisting at first of one superintendent and three police constables, possibly one of the earliest forces of its kind in England.

The mayor was chosen and sworn in annually on 'every Monday immediately before the feast of St Michael the Archangel', the first in October or last in September,

The Fire Brigade

The volunteer fire brigade was formed in the 18th century by the Kendal Fell Trust and was administered by the borough after 1835, with the police superintendent as captain. The brigade attended the devastating fire in 1829 at the extensive Dockwray Hall woollen mills beside the river in the northern part of the town. 700 packs of wool and all the valuable machinery were destroyed and the whole town seemed to have turned out to watch the flames. The heat of the fire boiled the water in the adjacent dam. The valiant efforts of the firemen were of no avail in preventing the total destruction of the mills, the loss being estimated at £20,000. A fire station was built in 1838 in

THE SITE OF KENDAL'S FIRST FIRE STATION 2005
K4710k (Trevor Hughes)

Finkle Street below the police office and the earliest appliances included buckets, hand-held squirts and a manually operated pump with leather hose in a hand-drawn watercart. The letters FP indicating fire plug (hydrant) can be seen inscribed on the building which is now shops.

when he customarily gave a banquet. The retiring mayor gave a similar banquet on the following Monday which was named Sergeant Monday. This became a general school holiday when boys followed the sergeants-at-arms in a noisy procession through the streets to the mayor's house where apples and other fruit were thrown from the window for the boys to scramble for. In later years the scramble took place outside the town hall, the custom surviving until the 1880s.

Did you know?

Nut Monday

Whole families went out into the woods and hedgerows on the public holiday in September to forage for nuts to augment their winter food supply. This custom fell out of favour by the 1860s and the holiday was abolished.

OLD SHAMBLES 2005 K4711k (Trevor Hughes)

which remains as a butcher's to this day. There were also cattle sales in the Market Place and a cattle fair was established on Beast Banks in 1816.

THE FAIR 2004 K4712k (Trevor Hughes)

Fairs on New Road, established by royal charter, are still held.

Animals were bought, sold and butchered on Beast Banks from an early date. A corporation byelaw made it an offence to kill a bull without first baiting it. The animal was secured to an iron ring and dogs were set on it to provoke it. The practice was a popular sport but was abolished in 1791. Butchers had moved from Beast Banks by 1785 into the newly built Old Shambles off Highgate. Problems with the draining of blood and offal caused a move again when Watt Lane between Market Place and Finkle Street was converted into the New Shambles. This soon became redundant with the opening of a municipal slaughterhouse and was changed into a delightful passage of shops, one of

Fairs had been a feature of Kendal life from the earliest days, and by the mid 19th century a regular pattern had developed of a spring fair at Whitsuntide and an autumn fair at Martinmas in November. An amusement fair is still held on similar dates to this day. Other fairs took place in various parts of the town, closely linked to the farming year. The horse fair along New Road, the potato, onion, damson or plum, the wool and cheese fairs were held mainly in the Market Place although some, like the damson fair, moved out into neighbouring streets. The noticeable width of Stramongate between Finkle Street and New Road still demonstrates a street designed for roadside marketing. The fairs held along New Road attracted travelling showmen, itinerant salesmen, pedlars and entertainers of all kinds. By the 1880s a full-scale entertainment fair

NOBLE'S YARD, 96, OFF STRICKLANDGATE 1914 67398x

The yards in Kendal were safe playgrounds for children.

had built up on the common land beside and even on the bed of the river. Perhaps most romantic were the hiring fairs held at Whitsun and Martinmas where men, women, boys and girls dressed in their best and crowded into Stricklandgate to seek work from farmers and others as servants for the coming half year. In some respects it was almost like a cattle show or slave market but both employers and employees looked at each other critically before either side agreed. The contract was usually sealed by the giving of a shilling and this was often spent by the boys before the end of the day on refreshment, an item of clothing, or at the fair where a fairing (ribbons or a trinket) might be bought for a sweetheart.

Childhood for ordinary children of the 'labouring classes' was short, most starting work at about 13 although many would have helped with domestic chores, farming work or helping father with his occupation at a much earlier age. Until the 19th century school was for the privileged few, either chosen for the Grammar School or the Bluecoat School, at private establishments for those whose parents could afford it, or with a governess or tutor at home. There were dame schools but these were generally little better than inefficient childminders, and even so cost precious pennies. In 1819 the first public day school (open to all children) in Kendal was opened for boys in a building designed by

George Webster in Lower Chapel Close north of All Hallows Lane at the foot of Beast Banks. It was incorporated with the National Society for promoting the education of the poor in the principles of the established church and was entitled the National School. It was founded by subscription and was endowed by Matthew Pyper of Whitehaven with £2,000. He requested that on his death he should be interred under the floor of the school, which he was. He was reinterred in the cemetery some time later. The emphasis of learning was on religious knowledge and 'works of industry', and attendance at Church of England festivals and Sunday services was mandatory. Slates were used for written exercises, supplemented by quill pens and paper for the older boys.

The school was successful and a girls' school was added in 1824 for instruction in reading, writing and the common rules of arithmetic and in singing, knitting and sewing. It is clear that both boys and girls were trained to fulfil their station in life. Society at the time was clearly stratified. This is exemplified in the now deleted verse of the children's hymn 'All Things Bright and Beautiful': 'The rich man in his castle, the poor man at his gate; God made them high or lowly and ordered their estate.' Everyone knew his place and generally accepted it. After a short experiment in Old Shambles in 1868 an infants' school joined the boys' and girls' schools. The schools changed in accordance with Education Acts and advances in the 1900s and closed in 1985,

THE GRAMMAR SCHOOL 1891 28622

housing being built on the site. However, the original plaque from the school doorway was retained and can still be seen.

By its very nature and constitution only those children whose families were prepared to comply with the conditions laid down by the National School could attend there. To cater for those who were not anglican in any way a committee from the Friends Meeting, the Quakers, opened a school under the auspices of the British and Foreign School Society to be run on non-denominational Christian principles. This was planned as an 'infant school for children aged from three to nine years of age from the labouring and manufacturing classes of society of every religious persuasion living in Kendal.' A neat schoolroom was built in 1830 in Castle Street near to Stock Beck Bridge by subscription from members of the Friends Meeting. The trustees were men and the school was administered by a committee of women. There was one mistress to teach as many as 60 children of all ages who each paid one or two pence per week, a common practice in such schools at that time. After a few years older girls up to the age of 13 were admitted and pupil teachers were indentured. In 1835 a separately founded and administered British School for boys was opened adjacent to the girls and infants and by 1863 all infant boys on reaching the age of seven were transferred to the boys' school. The school closed in 1968, by which time few children of school age lived in the catchment area. The boys' school building still stands in use for other purposes but the girls' and infants' school was demolished in the late

1990s and a 'school house' built on its site. A new Grammar School building was erected in The Lound near to Romney Bridge and was opened in 1889 by the Lord Mayor of London, the Rt Hon Sir James Whitehead, a Kendal boy made good. This school changed over the years and in 1980 took in the girls from the High School on Thorny Hills to form the present comprehensive Kirkby Kendal School.

A number of philanthropic persons were concerned for the poor and indigent. Dorothy Dowker in 1831 left a sizeable legacy to found a charity, known as Dowker's Hospital, to care for 'six females of good and chaste character born in Kendal, having attained the age of 50 years without being married.' They were housed in a Jacobean style building at the entrance to Abbot Hall Park in Highgate, designed by George Webster. It fell into disrepair in course of time and was demolished in 1963 to make the lane which bears the name of Dowker. Fortunately, the doorway was saved and re-erected at the top end of the Webster's Yard housing complex in Highgate. This bears a coat of arms showing six ducks, but no drake, an amusing reference to the spinsters.

John Sleddall, a descendant of Thomas Sleddall, Mayor of Kendal in 1636, planned to build almshouses at New Hutton but when he called on the local vicar to discuss the project he was kept waiting in a draughty corridor. Taking offence at this indignity he left the vicarage and decided to use his money elsewhere. He chose to exercise his charity in Kendal, and to commemorate Queen

Victoria's Golden Jubilee of 1887 had the almshouses built in Aynam Road that bear his name, leaving an endowment to provide a small income for the residents. A chapel for the residents was built at one end of the houses which in recent years was converted into more apartments.

SLEDDALL ALMSHOUSES 1896 38530

DOWKER'S HOSPITAL AND THE ENTRANCE TO ABBOT HALL PARK 1914 67371

The entrance to the park is on the right. On the low wall is a plaque recording the gift from the Kendal Savings Bank in 1897 towards the town's purchase of the park.

A report on the health of Kendal written by Dr Proudfoot in 1822 censured the town for its low standard of hygiene among the poorer classes resulting in illness, depression and premature death, the area around the parish church being the most unhealthy. Such criticism was also made about many another town of the time. The blame could not all be laid on the shoulders of the poor. Cramped lanes and yards, common privies, open sewers, impure water, ill ventilation and general dirt all combined to act against them. This situation remained unchanged for many years and cholera was prevalent. A board of health was set up, and in 1864 some gentlemen of the town decided to arrange for public wash-houses and baths to be built in All Hallows Lane. Designed by the local

architect Miles Thompson, they were fitted with the most modern laundry equipment with 22 washing stalls and eight bath rooms, six on the ground floor for men and two for women above them. At last there could be an end to damp washing hanging up in the already cramped living rooms and a real bath could be taken in private luxury.

A swimming pool was added in the 1880s to provide pleasurable relaxation and

EFFIGY OF MILES THOMPSON 2005 K4713k (Trevor Hughes)

A local architect of note, Miles Thompson is remembered by his effigy placed on a roof gable in Beast Banks by his brother Robert.

Did you know?
Cost of a Bath

The charges for baths for the labouring classes in the 1860s were: children not older than eight or more than four bathing together with one towel in a cold bath or shower 2d, or in a warm bath or shower 4d. Adults were charged 1d for the use of one towel in a cold bath or 2d in a hot one. Soap was supplied for one bath at 1d. Any person staying in the bath for longer than half an hour was charged double!

exercise. With further improvements in living conditions and the construction of a modern swimming pool in the leisure centre in the 1960s the wash-house and baths became redundant and were converted into district council offices, to be turned into a public house bearing the name of Miles Thompson at the beginning of the 21st century. New cemeteries were opened off Castle Street in 1843, and in Parkside Road in 1854 where Protestants and Catholics were segregated. A reservoir for supplying drinking water was opened in 1848 and water-closets became gradually widespread in houses. In one way or another the health of the town was improved out of all recognition.

In 1790 the Kendal Fell Trust fenced off a large area of its lands and planted trees

SERPENTINE WALKS 1914 67382

and shrubs. In 1824, through the efforts of some 40 subscribers, it laid out paths, erected a small summer house and planted flower beds to form Serpentine Walks as a pleasure resort where people could stroll round the wooded paths and picnic in the leafy glades on the payment of 6d admission. At Easter 1849 the grounds were thrown open freely to the public, Kendal's first municipal park, and in 1861 by an Act of Parliament they were dedicated permanently to public recreation. The walks, or woods as they are known today, proved popular although vandalism reared its ugly head even at that early time. Squirrels, owls and other birds were abundant and a large variety of wild flowers, some rare

The Time Gun

SERPENTINE WALKS, THE TIME GUN 1896 38537

The gun indicated 1pm Greenwich Mean Time each day and was first fired on 6th September 1873, by electricity, from T & E Rhodes, clockmakers, in Highgate. The Time Gun had come from HMS 'Warspite', a third-rater of 74 guns displacing 1,800 tons, built at Chatham in 1807 and cut down to a frigate in 1840. The gun was an 18-pounder, 9 feet long and weighing 2 tons 2 cwts. At one time complaints were made that it was too loud. It was repositioned and then people said they could not hear it! Having served its purpose well, when it wore out in 1908 it was replaced by a smaller gun which was fired until the outbreak of war in September 1939. It mysteriously disappeared in the 1940s and was not replaced since it was no longer needed.

or uncommon, could be seen and enjoyed though there is no record of a snake having ever been seen. There was a well which was reputed to have medicinal properties, the caretaker of the walks bottling and selling the water. Children called the summer house the cuckoo house from the sounds produced by shouting through the keyhole.

The Kendal Golf Club was founded in 1891, playing on the old race-course on Scout Scar. The Cunswick Golf Club had a nine-hole course on Cunswick Scar and moved to a new site on the Heights, near to Serpentine Walks, in 1897, changing its name in 1908 to the Serpentine Golf Club. A neat clubhouse of corrugated iron was erected in 1893 which had magnificent views over the mountains. In 1907 the two clubs combined as the Kendal Golf Club obtained more land from the Fell Trust. The club prospered, recording about a hundred members at the turn of the century and in 1907 turned down a motion to introduce play on Sundays. It is still going strong.

Transport was transformed during the beginning of the 19th century. In 1826 John Macadam, the advisor to the Turnpike Trusts, experimented with his newly devised road surface in Stricklandgate. In place of the earth tracks which were cut into ruts by carts and carriages, producing dust in dry and mud in wet weather, he prepared a solid foundation with drainage each side and built up the surface with small stones which were ground in by passing traffic to make a smooth roadway. The Kendal Chronicle grumbled that it was all right for turnpike roads but would never

do in towns and wished it had been tried on Shap Fell instead, but a correspondent rejoined that the newspaper was quite wrong as it was the best road ever invented. He was proved right and with the addition of tar the modern tarmac became universal. With better roads bicycles of various types came into use, became popular for work and pleasure, and were a common sight affording the benefit of a further range of travel to many of all social classes. Bicycles were ridden in many processions and competitions were organised for the best decorated.

FARRER'S TEA SHOP 2005
K4714k (Trevor Hughes Collection)

Established as a tea and coffee merchants in 1819, John Farrer's shop retains its Georgian appearance today.

The canal came to Kendal from Lancaster in 1819, the old Miller's Close Bridge across the river being rebuilt in 1818 in readiness to take the expected increase in traffic to the canal head basin. The formal opening was made a public holiday, the proceedings being watched by excited crowds, some thousand being estimated on Castle Hill. The canal marked a turning point in Kendal's prosperity, breaking down its insularity and providing easy access for trade with nearby towns, villages and further afield. Lower transport costs reduced the price of coal, limestone and slate both into and out of the town, a packet boat being introduced for passenger traffic. In later years suitably cleaned barges with seats were hauled by the horses taking children on Sunday school outings to Levens Park. At the edge of town beside the wharves a changeover bridge enabled the horses to change sides from one towpath to the other, and the marks of the ropes rubbing against the stonework can still be seen.

Progress is inevitable and in 1846, despite vigorous protests by William Wordsworth and others, the railway came from Oxenholme into Kendal amidst similar excitement to that which had greeted the canal. The bridge over Longpool beside the station was Kendal's first iron bridge and was only expected to last for 40 years, but is still in use! The railway, which was extended to Windermere, brought in new industries and revolutionised passenger travel. Trains were run for special occasions,

BRANTHWAITE BROW 1914 67383

such as to the Great Exhibition in 1851. During times of war embarking soldiers crammed the station and the surrounding roads were packed with patriotic crowds. Rail travel was naturally swifter than the horse-drawn barges and even the fastest packet boats, and the canal's fortunes began to decline. In 1864 it was leased by the London & North Western Railway which bought it outright in 1885. In 1948 the canal was nationalised and in 1955 was classified among those having insufficient commercial prospects to justify its retention, so it was closed and in the early 1960s the section to the borough boundary was filled with domestic and trade rubbish. This left the delightful Rennie bridges high and dry and provided a footpath where once people angled, bathed, skated and sometimes even committed suicide. As for the railway, its heyday too was over by 1968 in the face of increasing road competition. In the 1970s its goods traffic ended and the line was made into a single track with a diesel train shuttling between Oxenholme and Windermere.

Among other improvements in the town was the widening of Branthwaite Brow in 1853 to make a more satisfactory entrance into Market Place. This involved cutting away the fronts of a number of rickety houses on one side and facing them with one-inch thick cast iron plates, a very early and unusual use of this form of construction. Poor William Wilkinson had one fall down on to his feet 'lacerating them in a shocking manner.' The building named The Chocolate Shop bears the date 1657 but, although the houses are

Did you know?

Webb's Lettuce

Clarence Webb was a noted Kendal horticulturalist who was very interested in producing improved varieties of flowers and vegetables. In the First World War he tried without success to promote allotments for growing food. One of his greatest successes was 'Webb's Wonderful Lettuce' which is popular today for salads.

very old, this refers to the date of the first chocolate shop opened in London.

The Pump Inn stood at the head of Finkle Street from at least 1600 leaving only narrow paths on each side, one being Crock Lane. The inn took its name from the ancient town well at its rear. It became rundown and decrepit and even as early as 1777 there was a suggestion to pull it down and open up the street, but the inn soldiered on until a firm decision to close it was made in 1868. The building was bought by the corporation for £1,600 in 1876 and succumbed to demolition in 1879.

A drinking fountain from the side of a building in Crock Lane was moved to the riverside in Aynam Road. It bears the date of 1857 but was not installed until the following year; perhaps it was not thought worthwhile going to the expense of altering it.

The yards, characteristic of Kendal, developed from burgage plots running from the main streets and were usually named

THE FLEECE INN 1914 67372

Originally named the Golden Fleece, the classical reference of the name of the inn is clearly linked to the wool trade. The building with its overhanging first floor is the only remaining example of its kind in Kendal. Such buildings lined much of Highgate in earlier days. On the left is Clarence Webb's shop.

THE RAINBOW INN YARD, 32 HIGHGATE 1914 67389

from a feature in them like Two-seater Yard in Highgate where a seat for the weary was placed on each side of the entrance, or a business, like Post Office Yard, or Cumstey's Yard after the name of a firm of fat refiners, or from the owner or a prominent resident. Dr Manning's Yard off Highgate was so called after the doctor who lived and practised in the house at the head of the yard in the late 19th century. He was a surgeon at the county hospital. Before him the house and yard were owned

NOBLE'S YARD, 96, OFF STRICKLANDGATE 1914 67398

Each yard was a compact community in which people lived and worked. This yard was named after Dr Samuel Noble who lived and practised in Stricklandgate.

by George Braithwaite, a Quaker drysalter. In the yard were cottages and workshops, a ropeworks, dyeworks, tannery and a windmill for grinding oak bark for the tanners. Woollen warehouses later replaced the ropeworks. Gates at the heads of the yards were often closed at 10pm, not to keep invaders out but to keep the residents in at night.

Conditions in the yards were cramped with a lack of hygiene. A midden, one earth closet from which the night soil was taken to the river, one communal tap if water was not to be brought from the same source, all combined to produce health hazards despite the efforts of housewives to keep their homes and families clean and healthy. Disease, especially cholera, took its toll, although there were some who lived to a ripe old age. Fanny Cropper was very concerned about the poor, sick people who could not afford medical help and her husband, James, built the Memorial Hospital in her memory in 1869. With the growth of the town it proved inadequate and the County Hospital, designed by J F Curwen, was opened in 1908. This too was superseded by the Westmorland General Hospital on the southern edge of the town in 1991. The Cropper Memorial Hospital building still stands at the top of Captain French Lane, having become a children's nursery, but the County Hospital was replaced by a nursing home with the tower of the hospital incorporated into the design.

The Rev J W Barnes led a major restoration of the parish church which was closed for the purpose from 1850 to 1852, the congregation worshipping temporarily in St George's

Did you know?

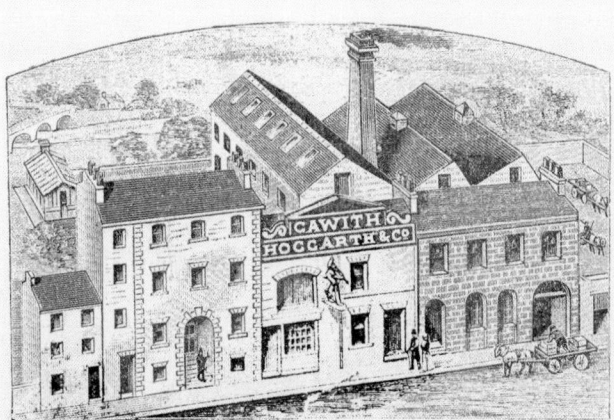

AN ENGRAVING OF THE SNUFF FACTORY FROM A LOCAL
GUIDE BOOK OF c1900 ZZZ04108
(Trevor Hughes Collection)

Snuff

Kendal is famous for Kendal Brown snuff, a powdered form of tobacco which was first ground in the town in the early 17th century. The second outbreak of plague in 1623 caused fewer deaths than the disastrous plague of 1598 and this was thought to be due to the use of snuff. Samuel Gawith was a well-known manufacturer whose offices in Lowther Street still have an effigy on the wall outside of a Turk, a common form of trade emblem for tobacconists.

THE PARISH CHURCH NAVE 1891 28617

Chapel in Market Place. The nave and chancel were virtually rebuilt, with the plaster and painting on the walls and pillars removed to reveal the old grey stone. A new and larger west door was built and new windows of stained and plain glass were installed. The old cramped, black, high-backed wooden pews were taken out with almost all the other woodwork. When the communicants returned they could hardly have recognised their new church. The increasing population required a new church at the northern end of the town and St Thomas's was built in 1837 at the foot of House of Correction Hill, almost opposite the Wesleyan chapel. The west end of the site by Dyers Beck where water and sewage drained from above proved too boggy to hold the weight of a tower, so the church was built in reverse with the

ST THOMAS'S CHURCH 1896 38534

The church was built by George Webster.

altar facing west instead of east. The two commissioners' churches, St Thomas's and St George's, together with Holy Trinity, now split the parish into three areas.

Kendal, like other towns, enjoyed street theatre with the religious mystery plays. These were opposed by the Puritans and were generally put down by the 1570s, but not in Kendal where the performance of the Corpus Christi play continued into the 17th century. At this time secular play-acting was born, producing such playwrights as Shakespeare, the plays being performed in available buildings like inns and even the moot hall. When the Civil War began in 1642 Parliament banned all public staging of plays but in the early 18th century they were again being performed in Kendal. The earliest theatre

or playhouse in the town was converted in 1758 from a part of what is now seen as the Working Mens' Institute in a corner of the Market Place. During the following 70 years other theatres were built, despite a general decline due in part to religious opposition. Then in 1828 two new theatres opened, one at the end of Old Shambles and the other in a yard next to the Bluecoat School. In addition the Shakespeare Inn was opened at the head of the yard. This was at a time when the Quakers were most influential in the town and the temperance movement had been formed. The Shakespeare Theatre, named after the inn, was closed after only a few years but the building remains, beautifully restored and used as a base by a community church while the inn still trades successfully.

The People's Palace

The Oddfellows Hall in Highgate experienced a brief moment of fame in 1890-91 when it became 'The People's Palace' to provide healthy, amusing entertainment and instruction for the working classes. It staged plays and other entertainments, lectures, lantern shows for children - 700 arrived for the 450 seats at the first performance - and classes for cookery, sewing, first aid, fencing and boxing, parlour games and the like, with a little magazine, 'The Kendalian'. It was highly popular but after closing for the summer failed to reopen. Other activities and possibilities for leisure and education had arisen which made it no longer needed, but it had, at least, shown the way for others to follow.

THE ODDFELLOWS HALL 2005 K4715k
(Trevor Hughes)

Cultural provision had been enhanced since Todhunter opened his first museum in Kirkland in 1792. In 1835 the Natural History and Scientific Society was founded, numbering among its first members William Wordsworth, Robert Southey, John Dalton and the geologist Adam Sedgwick. It moved to Stricklandgate House in 1854, changing its name to the Kendal Literary and Scientific Society and forming a library and museum. The museum was started with 'a few stuffed birds and one or two relics of antiquity' and grew gradually into an imposing and valuable collection, opening to the public without charge in 1900 to become a phenomenal success.

Patriotism reached its zenith towards the end of the 19th century, exemplified by the celebrations of Queen Victoria's Golden and Diamond Jubilees. The Golden Jubilee of 1887 was marked by the opening of a new market hall and a new Grammar School, each to replace an older one, and the opening of a new road between Stricklandgate and the railway station. Named Sandes Avenue after the philanthropist Thomas Sandes, it also included a new bridge over the river made of iron instead of stone, called Victoria or Jubilee Bridge. The opening of the bridge was a public holiday and brought a fine procession through the town. At the bridge there were the usual speeches and cheers, at the end of which four volleys were fired from cannons which broke a few windows, but this

A GENERAL VIEW LOOKING NORTH 1896 38526

Looking north, the iron Victoria Bridge is seen on the left centre with the stone Stramongate Bridge in front, almost hidden by trees. The spires of St George's Church are on the right.

was all taken in good part. The Jubilee also engendered the idea of a public library and progress on this was slow indeed. The passing of the Public Libraries Act was the spur, and the redundant old market hall was converted for the purpose, opening in 1892.

Celebrations in 1897 were even more extravagant, and coincided with the opening of a new Presbyterian church, St John's, in

Sandes Avenue. Much discussion took place by the corporation on ways to celebrate the Jubilee. From the many suggestions it was decided to stage a grand procession and to purchase Kendal Castle, Castle Hill and Abbot Hall and the park for public use and recreation, with the condition that no alcoholic drink be sold in the park. The mayor, corporation and representatives of the public bodies paraded to the parish church on Sunday 20th June for a special service of thanksgiving. The great day itself, the Tuesday, was a public holiday. The town was gaily decorated *en fête* and the town hall was illuminated by gas. A procession to rival all previous processions, reminiscent of the old guild parades, set off from Sandes Avenue to the town hall where the new clock and carillon of bells presented by the Mayor, Alderman Bindloss, to replace the old clock, were dedicated. The hands were set at 11 o'clock and the mayoress started the clock by pulling a string whereupon the bells immediately struck the hour. The bells today strike the hours and quarters and play a melody at intervals throughout the day, each day having its own tune. A large letter B for Bindloss can be seen under the clock faces. The name Bindloss is also commemorated by the Bindloss Room in the town hall, the recent extension of which was a gift from the Bindlosses.

The loyal address was read and the procession restarted round the town to the resounding cheers of the crowds. There was the customary luncheon, tickets three shillings for men and two and sixpence for women, where endless speeches were made. The children were presented with medals at their schools and all 3,551 of them made their way to Abbot Hall, the infants in waggons, for an *al fresco* tea and games followed by a march, four abreast, to Castle Hill where they had to endure a long speech before the gala. For six hours there was a programme of music by bands which accompanied dancing in the castle yard, running and novelty races,

wrestling, and pole leaping. There was a demonstration of jumping by the champion, Darby, who cleared 59 feet 2 inches in six back jumps. For the children there were ascents of character balloons and Punch and Judy shows. As darkness fell the castle was decorated with coloured lights and at 10pm the finest firework display ever seen at the castle began, including such delights as writhing cobras, fairy glowworms, giant rockets, aerial treasures of Sinbad's palace and the Niagara of fire, concluding with a colossal fire portrait of Queen Victoria and the words 'God Bless Her'. If that were not enough, the revellers streamed down to the park to dance until dawn. The celebrations ended on the Thursday with a treat for the aged people and widows of Kendal, where tea for about a thousand was followed by a two-hour entertainment. After the national anthem the women were given fruit cakes and the men tobacco. The Westmorland Gazette commented that, 'from the beginning to the end the Jubilee festivities passed over without a hitch or flaw of any kind.' They provided a very real boost to the morale and happiness of the ordinary working people of the town.

Hardly had the euphoria begun to fade when dark clouds began to form, signalling the outbreak of the second Boer War in 1899. Several hundred men from the town enrolled and joined the Kendal Volunteers to march to the station, to be transported on their way to South Africa to fight for queen and country, cheered on their way by patriotic Kendalians. So ended the 19th century and life was never to be the same again.

CHAPTER FOUR

Wars, Peace and Change

THE OPENING OF THE 20th century marked the end of an era and the beginning of a period of prolonged change. Queen Victoria was rapidly reaching the conclusion of her long reign and the Boer War was still raging. The atmosphere was decidedly gloomy. On 22 January 1901 the queen died and the whole country was plunged into mourning. Black was seen everywhere in Kendal and even the children wore black armbands. The accession of King Edward VII was proclaimed on a typically cold, wintry day outside the town hall and from the Call Stone in Market Place, and the schools were closed for the children to attend the solemn and historic occasion. On the day of the queen's funeral all business was suspended in the town and the mayor, with prominent local citizens, led a procession to the parish church for a service taking place at the same time as the official one in Windsor. Even the weather, dull and gloomy, befitted the occasion as large crowds lined the streets to mourn in silence their late queen, their royal mother. But life had to go on and a few months later the glad news was received that the Boer War was moving to its end. Jubilant crowds greeted the returning Kendal Volunteers with heroes' welcomes, the streets around the railway station being so packed that the soldiers had difficulty marching in line. 1902 promised a year of celebration as the coronation of the new king approached. Kendal was highly decorated, triumphal arches were constructed over roads and plans were made for a grand procession. Then came the sudden blow that the king was laid low with appendicitis, his life hanging in the balance. All the decorations save those at Abbot Hall were taken down but with the good news of his recovery were replaced and Kendal rejoiced in its usual patriotic way. The new century had at last begun in earnest.

Facing the approach to the railway station, the hotel was originally named the Railway Hotel. With the decline in the railway brought about by the motor car, the hotel changed its name.

THE COUNTY HOTEL 1924 75801

The motor car was beginning to make its mark. In April 1900 the Automobile Association ran a one-thousand mile trial with 65 cars taking part. The route taken was from Bristol via Carlisle to Edinburgh, returning via Newcastle to London, visiting as many cities as possible with an exhibition demonstrating the virtues of the new, exciting form of transport. Kendal, a small market town, was favoured by being included among

the big cities and the admission money to the exhibition was donated to the Boer War fund. 49 cars completed the trial which included the fierce Shap hills. It was won by the Hon Charles Stewart Rolls, of later Rolls Royce fame, in a 12 horsepower Panhard with a Daimler engine. In the town a speed limit of 8 mph was enforced on cars in the main roads in 1907; this was raised to 10 mph in 1910 and finally to the national 30 mph in 1935. There were no such limits on other forms of traffic and a judge in 1900 ruled that a pedestrian was entitled to walk as he wished on the queen's highway; a cyclist who ran down a man instead of avoiding him was fined 30 guineas! Bicycles were still the common form of transport for the ordinary person; no less than 574 were counted at a demonstration at Levens Bridge. Traffic problems began to grow as early as 1912 when cars parked in Highgate caused a dangerous obstruction. Traffic wardens were introduced in 1967 and one caused a furore by issuing a ticket on a fire engine parked on a double line while attending a fire! A one-way system was established through the town in 1968 to ease the flow of traffic and in 1971 a bypass was constructed, though many complained that it was on the wrong side of the town to be of any real use. Neither of these schemes was the answer to alleviating the effects of the increasing traffic and inconvenience.

HIGHGATE 1914 67368

A line of electric tramway was proposed in 1900 to run from the railway station via Finkle Street to Highgate and then to Nether Bridge, with a branch to the Wesleyan church in Stricklandgate. This was in conjunction with plans to bring an electricity supply into the town in 1902. It was suggested that, if the tramway proved unsuccessful, the posts supporting the overhead wires could be used as lamp posts. However, nothing came of the tramway plan. Another abortive suggestion, in the 1930s, was to build an aerodrome for the town. Captain Elwell of Morecambe had raised interest when he conducted passenger flights over Kendal from Longlands in 1925, the charge being 7s 6d.

KENDAL KOMET ADVERTISEMENT 1901
ZZZ04109 (Trevor Hughes Collection)

WIPER & RUTTER ADVERTISEMENT FROM A TOWN GUIDE BOOK OF 1909 ZZZ04110 (Trevor Hughes Collection)

The time had come in 1907 for the ancient township of Kirkland to lose its separate status. The Kendal Corporation Bill sought to transfer powers from the Kendal Fell Trustees, to unite all the townships within the borough into one parish and, among other matters, to equalise the various rates imposed. The bill received the royal assent on 26 July and the folllowing year Kendal was now one borough, although the good folk of Kirkland still regarded themselves, with all their history and traditions, as a race apart.

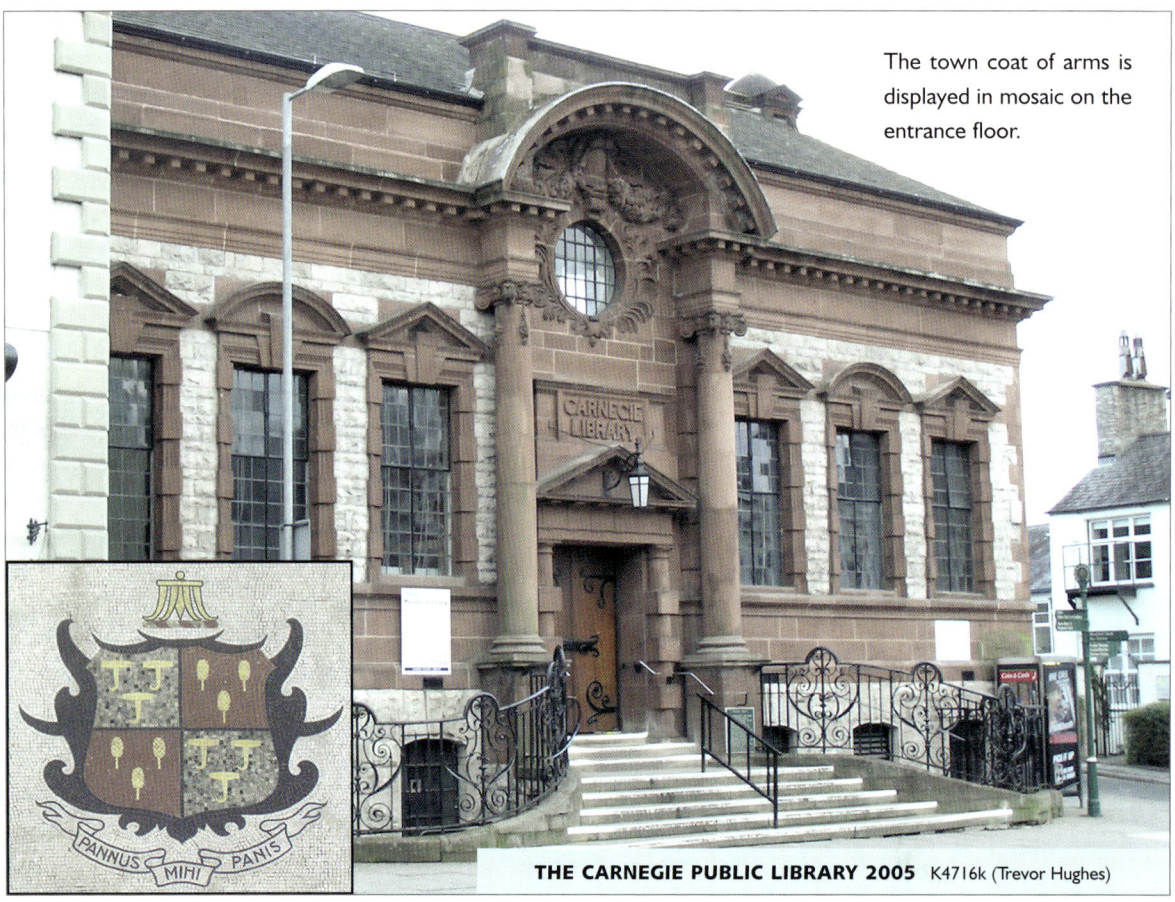

The town coat of arms is displayed in mosaic on the entrance floor.

THE CARNEGIE PUBLIC LIBRARY 2005 K4716k (Trevor Hughes)

Another institution to see change was the free public library in Stricklandgate. It had been established in the old market hall in 1892 as an offshoot from the Golden Jubilee celebrations and had proved an instant success. After some fifteen years it was showing that it had served its purpose but was now too small and was only ever a makeshift arrangement. In 1906 Andrew Carnegie, the American philanthropist, promised £5,000 for a new building and this provided the impetus for change. The new library was built in uncharacteristic Penrith red sandstone on the opposite side of Stricklandgate and was named after its benefactor. It was opened on 20 March 1909 by the mayor who stood in for Carnegie's representative, Dr Morrison of Edinburgh, who had injured his back by falling from a tramcar. The old library was summarily demolished and the stonework was bought by Thompson Bros who used it to form a warehouse in front of their Duckett Printing Works in Sandes Avenue. The front and two adjacent sides of the old library - there was no plain back to it - were laid out in one straight line by the architect, John Thompson, in a design very similar to the original appearance except that the pediment was cut into pieces and used in the basement to help support the weight of the structure. The building, containing the old library clock, remains intact to this day.

The opening of the new free public library had a damaging effect on the Kendal Literary and Scientific Institution, causing it to be disbanded in 1913. Its museum in Stricklandgate was closed and some of the more valuable treasures were sold to the British Museum (Natural History) in London, the left over exhibits being handed to the corporation as a nucleus of a town museum. This museum was eventually opened in 1918 in Albert Buildings opposite the station, Whitwell Hargreaves and Company's old Northern Counties' Wool Warehouse, where it still contains a fascinating range of displays about the town.

KENDAL MUSEUM 2005 K4717k (Trevor Hughes)

There was a proposal to use Stricklandgate House as a cinema but this came to nothing. However, the cinema was destined to come to Kendal. John W Hewitson's boot warehouse in Sandes Avenue closed down and was converted into a picture house in 1913, the Kendal Kinema, which was opened by the mayor and mayoress in July the same year. As its origin would suggest, both exterior and interior were box-like and unprepossessing but this did not put people off. Together with the usual drama films there were moving pictures of local events in the town, including scenes of workers leaving the mills where great enjoyment was had in picking out one's own face and those of friends and well-known people. At the time the Kinema with its red plush seats and carpeted floor was considered the acme of luxury. It was well patronised, a pianist being employed to play appropriate music for the silent films, and noisy boys read out the captions to those who could not read; sound came in 1928. The cheap seats were usually occupied by women; young lads often waited until the house lights were dimmed before moving to more expensive seats. In 1920 the Kinema changed its name to the Super Picture House and in 1937 to the Roxy, perhaps hoping to throw off its nickname of the Flea Pit; attendants used regularly to spray 'Keating's Kills' disinfectant down the aisles during the intervals.

A second cinema opened in 1931, the Palladium, also in Sandes Avenue, converted from the Handle factory. It was an imposing place with all the most modern equipment and smart usherettes. The screen was covered by heavy brown curtains when live performances were staged. From the start it showed talking pictures and was so superior to the Roxy that it caused it to close in 1960. At the Palladium all was not well during the jive dance craze of the 1950s. When the Bill Haley and the Comets' film, 'Rock Around the Clock', was shown there were riotous scenes with youths in teddy-boy suits and girls in dirndl skirts jiving and clapping up and down the aisles, chanting to the music. The police had to be called to eject them whereupon they continued dancing

ST GEORGE'S CHURCH 1888 21089

The magnificent towers and spires became dangerous and had to be removed.

and chanting in the street until the police restored order. Kendal was not alone in this as similar scenes occurred in cinemas all over the country. During their customary inspection in 1986 the fire brigade identified a string of defects and safety hazards which led to the closure of the cinema. So ended the reign of the dedicated cinema in the town although films were still shown in St George's Theatre in Stramongate, and are still shown to this day in the Brewery Arts Centre.

War clouds gathered again in 1914 when the First World War, the Great War, broke out. Universal excitement greeted the call to arms. The Territorial Army was called back from its summer camp at Caernarfon and K-Shoes received an order for 400 pairs of boots. Swarms of men, young and old, rushed to join in the big adventure, which was confidently expected to be over by Christmas, and they were drilled in Kendal Castle yard. As the volunteer recruits marched to the railway station they were cheered and jostled by the patriotic crowds lining Wildman Street and the station approach. It was common practice, certainly in the northern towns, to post men from the same town together as 'pals' and Kendal was no exception. By 1915 there were 1,200 Kendal pals who marched, fought and died together. As the war dragged on to the accompaniment of ritual slaughter The Westmorland Gazette published a growing list of casualties with pages of photographs of the gallant lads who had perished or were missing. A Voluntary Aid Detachment (VAD) hospital was set up in the Friends School in Stramongate to care for wounded soldiers, and a team of ladies repaired their linen and uniforms. Over at the public baths in All Hallows Lane washerwomen cleaned their clothes and the soldiers were allowed to use the baths free of charge. Tobacco, mint cake, toffee, chocolate, cake, bootlaces, socks and candles were collected and made up into parcels to send to soldiers on the front. The armistice came at last, and the dead were honoured with their 316 names inscribed on a cenotaph war memorial erected in 1921 on the site of the old library in Market Place facing Stricklandgate. A large company attended the opening, with a contingent of children dressed in white singing hymns with the crowd to the accompaniment of a portable organ mounted on a cart. In 1919 Kendal corporation was presented with war trophies for safe care and custody.

MARKET PLACE AND THE WAR MEMORIAL 1921 70684x

War Trophies

Kendal's war trophies consisted of a German tank, a captured German heavy gun and a fifteen-inch shell. The tank was given by the War Savings Association and, after initial fears that Stramongate Bridge would not carry its weight, it was installed on Miller Green, near the end of Miller Bridge. It was sold for scrap in 1937. The shell was offered to Kendal museum and the gun was placed in Abbot Hall Park alongside the original Time Gun which had been fitted with a carriage. The guns were a popular display, especially for small boys, and for many years fostered military patriotism. When war broke out again in 1939 they were taken away as scrap metal for the war effort.

THE OLD TIME GUN IN ABBOT HALL PARK
ZZZ04111 (Trevor Hughes Collection)

The armistice was only a pause in hostilities which erupted again in September 1939 as the Second World War. There was not the same rush to join up this time and conscription was brought in fairly soon. Apart from those involved, killed or wounded in the actual conflict, Kendal was less affected than in the previous war, apart from rationing, blackout, gas masks and other irritants. As with the previous war The Westmorland Gazette listed those killed, injured and missing and included photographs but the carnage was nothing like that of the Great War.

Evacuees were received at the beginning of the war from Newcastle and South Shields and by December 38% of the total had returned home. A further evacuation of children, this time from the south, came to Westmorland, many of them staying in centres where they rested before moving on; some 500 were housed in Kendal. When peace returned there was great jubilation with street parties, services of thanksgiving in the churches, the joy of receiving back the homecoming fathers, and general relief. The town was bedecked with flags and decorations and there was dancing in Abbot Hall Park. Remembrance Day services were held each year afterwards at the war memorial followed by the parading of the mayor, corporation and public services to the parish church.

Compared with the larger towns and cities Kendal is a peaceful town so it is understandable that two dreadful crimes rocked the community. The first occurred in 1904 in a house in Woolpack Yard where the 83-year-old John Gilpin died in suspicious circumstances. A post mortem showed arsenic in his body and his housekeeper, Elizabeth Nicholson, and a lodger, Thomas Metcalf, were charged with murder. As the case proceeded a sorry tale unfolded. Gilpin had taken up with Elizabeth over 20 years before and his family had disowned him. When he became senile Thomas moved in and formed an alliance with Elizabeth. The Mayor of Kendal, John Monkhouse, knew all about this and ignored it, failing as his trustee to discover that Thomas had been forging Gilpin's signature on cheques. Thomas had bought arsenic from a local chemist and it was alleged that he arranged for it to be put

THE WOOLPACK YARD 2005 K4718k (Trevor Hughes)

The archway of the old Woolpack Inn was high enough to allow waggons piled with bales of wool to pass through.

into Gilpin's rum. The case took three days before the jury, after an absence of only six minutes, returned its verdict. Elizabeth was convicted of murder and Thomas of aiding and abetting. A crowd waited for them for three hours outside the town hall and lined the whole road to Oxenholme station to watch them being taken to the Lancaster assizes. There, to everyone's surprise, the case against Thomas was dropped and Elizabeth was found not guilty. Although the jury had, at first by a small majority, held her guilty they decided in the end that it was not fair for her to be hanged while Thomas got off scot-free. How strange are the minds of men.

A second murder took place in 1915 on the Kendal golf course where the green keeper found a milliner's assistant named Lily Hadwin lying dead at the foot of Scout Scar. Private Musweek, her boyfriend, was arrested and charged with pushing her over the edge of the escarpment. The defence insisted that she might have slipped or taken her own life and the evidence was considered inconclusive so he was cleared, but the police were not convinced. Their representative is on record as saying that, in his opinion, he only got away with the crime because there was a war on and as a soldier he was of more use to the country as cannon fodder. Morbid crowds flocked to see the place where her body was found although there was really nothing there to see.

The Golf Links Murder was the news of the day in 1915.

THE VIEW FROM THE GOLF LINKS c1925 K4308

Did you know?

Mint Cake

It is said that Joseph Wiper was the first to make Kendal mint cake although others claim that honour. It is a combination of sugar, glucose and peppermint and is a favourite with walkers, athletes and mountaineers as it gives energy quickly. Hillary and Tensing took it to the summit of Everest in 1953, and Dr Somervell of Kendal in 1924 presented some to the Lama of Tibet during the ill-fated expedition when Mallory and Irvine were fatally lost.

The Original

Kendal Mint Cake

*T*HERE *are several local confections known as " Kendal Mint Cake," and visitors are often misled, and buy any kind of Mint Cake under the assumption that it is the Original Confection which was supplied to*

The Imperial Trans Antarctic Expedition 1914-1917 (passed by War Office Food Experts Whitehall).

The Mount Everest Expeditions 1922, 1924.
The Algarsson North Polar Expedition 1925.
and eaten by thousands of our Soldiers and Sailors during

The South African War 1899-1902,
The Great War 1914-1918,

and which has become famous throughout the world for its delicate, refreshing qualities and flavour. (see page 17).

All the Mint Cake used on the above Expeditions was manufactured by, and bears the name

ROBERT WIPER

on every packet.   Obtainable from all best Confectioners.

When purchasing—refuse all imitations.

ROBERT WIPER'S
Original Kendal Mint Cake.

If any difficulty in securing, please advise
R. WIPER, Wholesale Confectioner,
" Gazette" Yard,   KENDAL.

MINT CAKE ADVERTISEMENT FROM A TOWN GUIDE BOOK OF 1926
ZZZ04112 (Trevor Hughes)

STEELE'S YARD, 123 HIGHGATE 1914 67393

YARD 59, STRAMONGATE 1914 67387

The years following the end of the Second World War were times of austerity and when the 1960s dawned all thoughts were on clearing away the old and starting a brave new world of hope and prosperity. Fellside was a running sore. On the steep slope between Kendal Fell and the river valley it was a crowded mass of old houses and cottages, the slums of the town, the 'ghetto of Kendal's poor', dating back to the 16th century. It was a wilderness of steep steps, terraces and ginnels in which it was easy to become lost. The Syke was a lane that ran down through the centre. The opportunity was used to undertake a wholesale demolition of property, replacing it all with modern housing. The inhabitants were rehoused in one or other of the council estates that had been built for the growing town. There is no doubt that a serious health hazard had been removed and that living conditions for those displaced were infinitely better, but a close community had been split up, to be replaced by a sterile locale devoid of the old attractive character. Names of some of the lanes and alleys were retained and just one of the old public houses was saved, the Hyena, converted into a house.

Fellside was a maze of steep little lanes and ginnels.

FOUNTAIN BROW, FELLSIDE 1914 67396

Did you know?

The T-Well

The well on Fellside provided a main public water supply and housewives met there to gossip. They said the water made the best cup of tea in Kendal. The name 'T-Well' comes from the common expression, 't'well' – the well. Despite its reputation, the water was dirty and disease-ridden and was a main cause of the illnesses, especially cholera, that plagued the people of Fellside.

It was not only Fellside that succumbed to the efforts of town planners; the yards were also affected, many being severely truncated and others completely lost in a flurry of removing old and unhygienic housing where changes in trades and occupations had made many of the buildings redundant. Dr Manning's Yard was saved and restored and Collin Croft, also off Highgate, remains to show, in sanitised form, something of how the yards once looked when they were a hive of activity. At the top end of the Croft it ascends by a series of steps to Beast Banks. It retains its cobbled roadway and was lovingly restored by the Kendal Civic Society, receiving a Civic Trust Award for the work in 1982.

The Kendal Civic Society was formed in 1963 with as its aim to 'preserve the best of the past; promote the best of the new.' It embarked on an ambitious programme

DR MANNING'S YARD, HIGHGATE 1914   67397

Did you know?

Collin Croft

This ancient yard was first named in an indenture of 1701. It contained the usual cottages and at various times housed warehouses, a timber yard, an iron founder, a blacksmith, a stonemason, stables, a coach builder, a beer house called the Malt Shovel, and many more trades. By 1879 the cottages had become greatly overcrowded and sanitary conditions were deplorable but it was a century before improvements were made.

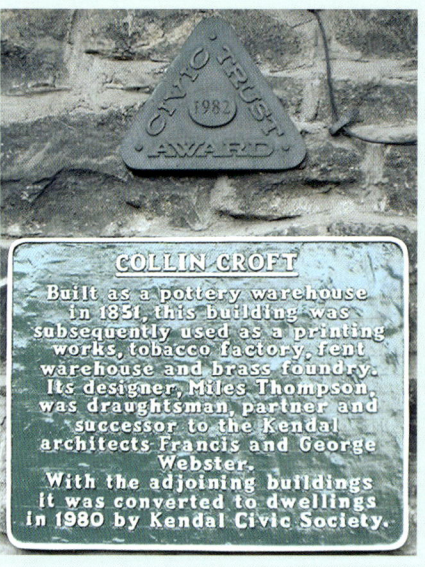

ABOVE: A CIVIC SOCIETY PLAQUE IN COLLIN CROFT 2005   K4719k (Trevor Hughes)

LEFT: COLLIN CROFT 1914   67384

involving street improvement schemes, building conservation projects and traffic studies. It engaged in an attempt to save from destruction New Bank Yard off Highgate, one of the best of the traditional yards, but lost the battle. Undeterred, the society went on to form a preservation trust which not only restored Collin Croft but also Pembroke House in Kirkland and the Summer House in Serpentine Woods, and rescued the near-derelict Shakespeare Theatre. It also shared in the cost of re-siting the Romney Suspension footbridge to a position at Dockwray when a new traffic bridge replaced it. The society

THE FLOOD 2004 K4720k (Trevor Hughes)

is very much the eyes and ears of the town, keeping a careful watch on developments affecting the conservation area. It has placed its well-known green plaques which give concise information for residents and tourists alike on over 50 historic buildings and sites throughout the town. In addition to its other publications it has produced a set of cards amplifying each plaque.

From the earliest times the River Kent has been prone to flooding. It drops some 2,000 feet in its 20-mile journey from the fells near High Street and is one of the swiftest flowing rivers in the country. Its level rises dramatically after heavy rain. The earliest flood recorded was on the 18 October 1635 when the wooden Miller's Close bridge was washed away. An even worse flood occurred on 11 September 1671 when the river level rose eight feet and swept over the churchyard wall where 'itt left much ffish'. It forced up the oak floor of the vestry and the churchwardens paid a group of men 1s 6d for drink when they had removed the church chest out of reach of the water. 13 October 1771 saw severe weather over the whole of the north of England and the parish church was involved again, with the river waters tearing up graves in the churchyard and entering the Friends Meeting House to such an extent that the worshippers

ST GEORGE'S CHURCH 1914 67377

had to evacuate the building. The following year Nether Bridge, which had only been widened three weeks before to cope with the increased traffic, was washed away and had to be rebuilt quickly, this time with better workmanship. Another major flood occurred on 8 February 1831 when the river rose over 21 inches in one day, being nearly seven feet deep over Colonel's Walk near the church. In 1861, on 26 November, the wooden bridge across the mill-race below Castle Mills was carried away bodily, and on 6 October 1874 the river rose even higher at 33 inches in just 24 hours, the worst flood known up to that time. The water washed through Wilkinson's dye works and flooded the bottom end of the town with an angry yellow surge. The lower part of Stramongate and the whole of Gooseholme were completely submerged, and the wooden bridge there was washed to the other side of the river. St George's Church stood as in the centre of a lake. But worse was to come. There was torrential rain all day and night on 2 November 1898 and by the following morning the river had spread far and wide beyond its banks, the worst flood in living memory, a good 15 inches above the level of 1874. The waters reached right to the tops of the arches of the bridges and in the area around Stramongate Bridge whole streets and hundreds of houses, shops, factories, schools and other buildings were inundated. Stramongate was under water from the bridge to the bottom of Blackhall Yard, while the flood extended along Wildman Street to Longpool. There were fears that St George's Church might be badly affected but in the event, ironically, the water only got into the hydraulic chamber. At the Castle Street girls' and infants' school the teachers attempted to keep the school running normally, but by 11am they and some parents had to carry children out to safety through several inches of water. The school was flooded to the depth of two feet, spoiling some of the new decoration. When the waters had subsided almost as quickly as they had risen there came the unenviable task of mopping up and cleaning. A slate plaque on Riverside shows the flood levels up to that year. There were floods in most years afterwards, Aynam Road being particularly affected, although not as severely, 1927 and 1954 being two of the worst. In the latter year at least 500 houses and shops were damaged. A wooden garage containing two cars was moved bodily 40 feet and swans swam in the water in the streets. The river found a new temporary channel from Nether Bridge along Lound Road, rejoining its normal course at Natland Road. The waters subsided by the end of the afternoon and hundreds of householders were left to clear up the mud and debris. A flood relief scheme in the 1970s was effective, although minor floods still occur occasionally.

Many personalities visited Kendal over the years. Buffalo Bill brought his Wild West Show in 1904 on its final tour of Britain. He came in three special trains for a one-day performance among the excitement of which were an enactment of the Battle of the Little Big Horn and Custer's Last Stand. At the other end of the spectrum, having completed an evangelistic campaign in the Holy Land and Australasia, General Booth, leader of the Salvation Army, came to Kendal in 1905. He came by car looking tired and careworn to St George's Hall where he attended a meeting. The main streets were lined by spectators to cheer him, and as he passed the local branch of the Army its band played 'We Lift the Banner High.' In 1908 half a dozen women from Newnham College in Cambridge, in heavy rain, gave speeches in Market Place to a large crowd advocating the cause of votes for women. A resolution was put to the meeting, carried unanimously and a grand collection was raised when a hat was passed round. On this occasion there was no chaining to railings or public uproar. Kendalians are in the main peace-loving and accepting people. King George V paid a surprise visit by car in 1911 to loud cheers from the crowds lining the streets as he passed slowly through the town without stopping. He noted particularly the cheers and flag-waving of the children for whom it was a red letter day. A further royal visit came in 1956 when the town was highly decorated for Queen Elizabeth II. Welcome arches were set up across the Windermere Road and the Milnthorpe Road at Helsington Laithes through which she passed. Kendal's weather lived up to its reputation when, after two days of glorious sunshine, the great day was marked with a deluge of rain but this did not deter the hardy souls who took their places soon after midnight to secure a good vantage point from which to see her majesty.

Alfred Wainwright

AW, as he was known, became inspired by a visit to the Lake District in 1930 and came to love its mountains, walking among them whenever he could. In 1941 he moved to Kendal where he worked in the borough treasurer's office, now within easy reach of the fells. He spent much of his spare time walking and sketching them, eventually producing the first of his guides to the fells. These were both hand-written and drawn in his inimitable style and have proved invaluable to walkers ever since. He was a very private man who preferred to walk alone with his thoughts. For a time he was the curator of Kendal museum, and towards the end of his life gave much of his book royalties to the charity Animal Rescue. He died at the age of 84 having left an invaluable legacy to fell walkers.

A SLATE PANEL OF A PAGE FROM AN ALFRED WAINWRIGHT BOOK 2005 K4721k (Trevor Hughes)

The rain stopped at about 11.30am and the streets suddenly became alive with cheering crowds along the roads closed to other traffic. Her Majesty spent nearly two hours in the town, lunching at the county hall. She was one of only three monarchs actually to set foot in Kendal, the previous being Charles II as far back as 1657.

The 20th century ending, the town set about welcoming the new millennium with customary enthusiasm, justifying a survey of 189 towns in Britain where it was ranked third against Dumfries and Livingston in Scotland. It was commended for its good level of health care and low crime rate and outdid picture-postcard places like York, Bath, Chester and Stratford-on-Avon. In contrast, Lancaster was listed 33rd and Barrow 140th. The general comment, well-deserved, was that 'Kendal is the finest town in England.'

ORDNANCE SURVEY MAP OF KENDAL c1897

CHAPTER FIVE

New Millennium, Bright Future

WITH OVER 1,000 years of history behind it, the town of Kendal stepped into the new century with confidence and resolute hope. The new hospital was now well established and showing its excellence of care. The cricket, rugby and football clubs, the annual Mary Wakefield music festival, the leisure centre and the Brewery Arts Centre provide for the physical, literary, artistic and cultural needs of all ages.

THE VIEW FROM QUEEN'S ROAD c1925   K4304

THE BREWERY ARTS CENTRE 2005
K4722k (Trevor Hughes)

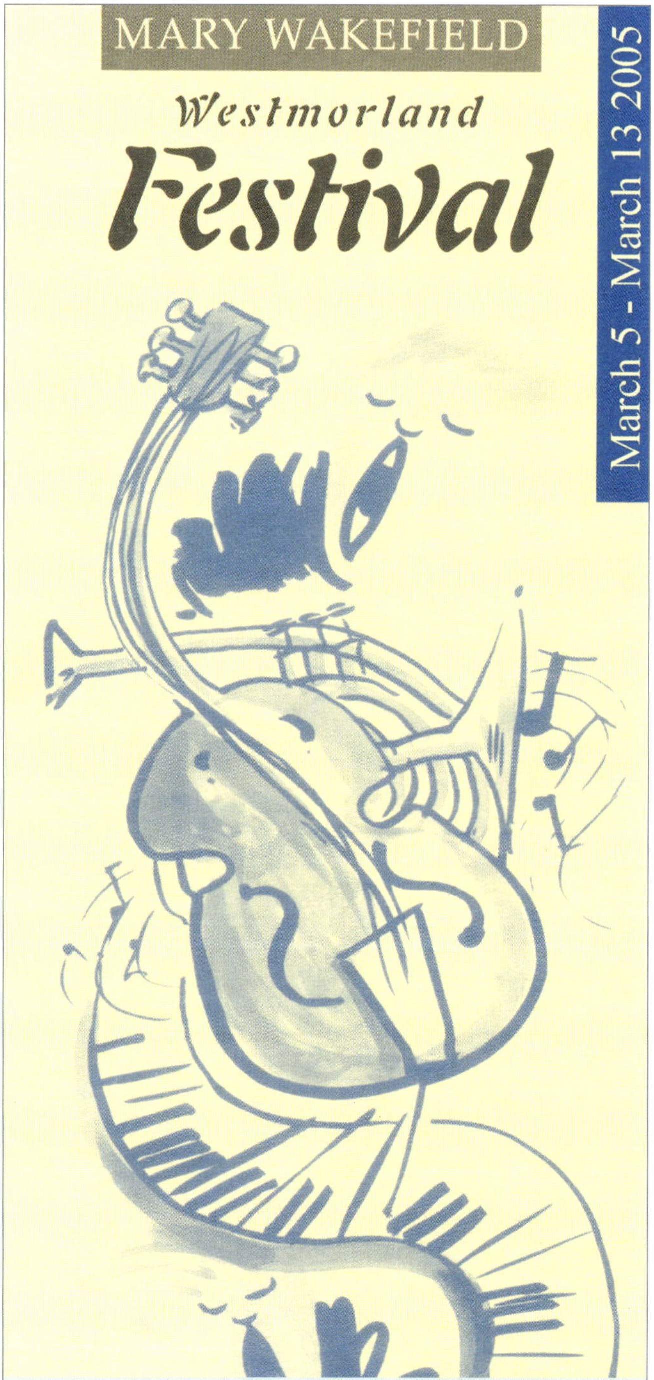

MARY WAKEFIELD

Westmorland

Festival

March 5 - March 13 2005

MARY WAKEFIELD WESTMORLAND FESTIVAL LEAFLET 2005
ZZZ04143 (Reproduced by kind permission of the secretary of the
Mary Wakefield Festival Committee)

**THE RINTELN PLAQUE
2005** K4723k (Trevor Hughes)

Kendal is twinned with Rinteln in Germany.

**THE OLD
GREENSIDE POST
OFFICE 2005** K4724k
(Trevor Hughes)

Alfred Wainwright, who wrote and illustrated the celebrated guide books to the Lakeland fells, and John Cunliffe, author of the popular children's stories about Postman Pat, both hailed from Kendal. This Post Office was used by John Cunliffe in his Postman Pat books for children.

Restoration of the canal has begun with Change Bridge.

CHANGE BRIDGE 2005   K4725k (Trevor Hughes)

The town boasts not one but two excellent museums and a renowned art gallery. The Kendal museum of archaeology, local and natural history has fascinating dioramas of animals set in surroundings depicting different habitats near at hand and around the world. There is also an interactive exhibit putting life into Kendal Castle whose sombre grey ruins watch over the town. The Museum of Lakeland Life and Industry carries interest into the wider community. The public library has a comprehensive archive of local interest. New projects are underway. The Kendal-Lancaster Canal which died and was buried in the 1960s is slowly but surely being brought back to life.

THE BIRDCAGE, FINKLE STREET 2005 K4726k (Trevor Hughes)

Kendal has so much now to offer its people and the tourists who flock to the 'Auld Grey Town'. The shelter at the head of Finkle Street, dubbed 'the Birdcage,' is a popular venue for promoting local and national issues, often with exciting music heard above the noise of traffic. The Westmorland Show held at Crooklands is awaited with eager anticipation during the Kendal Gathering each September, a place where town and country meet to enjoy animal displays and competitions and the vast array of stalls with their many attractions. The old wash-houses and baths have been pleasingly converted into a public house and given the name of the local architect who designed the buildings, Miles Thompson.

For those who delight in retail therapy there are the Westmorland Shopping Centre and the Elephant Yard shopping mall, both of which display a mix of local and national high street shops. Markets are held on Wednesdays and Saturdays and a farmers' market is held monthly on a Friday. The new supermarket hides its delights behind the shops of Stricklandgate.

MARKET PLACE 2005 K4727k (Trevor Hughes)

The markets continue the age-old tradition.

WAINWRIGHT'S YARD PLAQUES 2005 K4728k
(Trevor Hughes)

BOOTHS SUPERMARKET 2005 K4729k (Trevor Hughes)

The latest supermarket development commemorates Alfred Wainwright, with a yard named after him.

Kendal is proud of its history and its attractive old grey stone buildings, described on the Civic Society plaques, but is not set in the past. It looks to the future and the future is bright. Kendal is a pleasant place in which to live, a market town that is busy and bustling yet has in its yards and alleys places of peace and tranquillity with specialist shops and cafés to delight and please.

THE TOWN HALL 2005 K4730k (Trevor Hughes)

The letter B under the clock refers to William Bindloss. He was three times Mayor of Kendal and was a generous benefactor to the town.

ACKNOWLEDGEMENTS

The authors are grateful for the help and encouragement given so freely by fellow local historians. Thanks are due to the staff of the Cumbria Record Office in Kendal, to the local studies section of Kendal public library and to those who, over the years, have shared their experiences and reminiscences.

BIBLIOGRAPHY

'A Boke off Recorde of the Burgh of Kendale', 1575
'A Celebration of 800 Years of Market Kendal', 1989
'Discover Kendal', A R Nicholls 2004
'Historic Kendal', J T Hughes 2005
'Kendal's Canal', J Satchell 2000
'Kendal Castle - A Guide', 2000
'Kendal on Tenterhooks', J Satchell 1984
'Kendal, A Social History', R Bingham 1995
'Kendal Past and Present' J Marsh 2003
'Kirkby Kendal', J Curwen 1900
'Local Chronology from Kendal Newspapers', 1865
'The Annals of Kendal', C Nicholson 1861
'The Kendal Weaver', J Satchell 1986
'Westmorland Gazette - A Book of the 20th Century', 2000

Minutes of Kendal Corporation and other Bodies
Local Newspapers

Ottakar's Bookshops

Ottakar's bookshops, the first of which opened in Brighton in 1988, can now be found in over 130 towns and cities across the United Kingdom. Expansion was gradual throughout the 1990s, but the chain has expanded rapidly in recent years, with many new shop openings and the acquisition of shops from James Thin and Hammicks.

Ottakar's has always known that a shop's local profile is as important, if not more important, than the chain's national profile, and has encouraged its staff to make their shops a part of the local community, tailoring stock to suit the area and forging links with local schools and businesses.

Local history has always been a strong area for Ottakar's, and the company has published its own award winning local history titles, based on text written by its customers, in recent years.

With a reputation for friendly, intelligent and enthusiastic booksellers, warm, inviting shops with an excellent range of books and related products, Ottakar's is now one of the UK's most popular booksellers. In 2003 and then again in 2004 it won the prestigious Best Bookselling Company of the Year Award at the British Book Awards.

Ottakar's has commissioned The Francis Frith Collection to create a series of town history books similar to this volume, as well as a range of stylish gift products, all illustrated with historical photographs.

Participating Ottakar's bookshops can be found in the following towns and cities:

Aberdeen	Douglas, Isle of Man	Kendal	St Helier
Abergavenny	Dumfries	King's Lynn	Salisbury
Aberystwyth	Dundee	Kirkcaldy	Sheffield
Andover	East Grinstead	Lancaster	Stafford
Ashford	Eastbourne	Lincoln	Staines
Ayr	Elgin	Llandudno	Stevenage
Banbury	Enfield	Loughborough	Sutton Coldfield
Barnstaple	Epsom	Lowestoft	Teddington
Basildon	Falkirk	Luton	Tenterden
Berkhamsted	Fareham	Lymington	Tiverton
Bishop's Stortford	Farnham	Maidenhead	Torquay
Boston	Folkestone	Maidstone	Trowbridge
Brentwood	Glasgow	Market Harborough	Truro
Bromley	Gloucester	Milton Keynes	Tunbridge Wells
Bury St Edmunds	Greenwich	Newport	Twickenham
Camberley	Grimsby	Newton Abbot	Walsall
Canterbury	Guildford	Norwich	Wilmslow and
Carmarthen	Harrogate	Oban	Alderley Edge
Chatham	Hastings	Ormskirk	Wells
Chelmsford	Haywards Heath	Petersfield	Weston-super-Mare
Cheltenham	Hemel Hempstead	Portsmouth	Windsor
Cirencester	High Wycombe	Poole	Witney
Coventry	Horsham	Redhill	Woking
Crawley	Huddersfield	St Albans	Worcester
Darlington	Inverness	St Andrews	Yeovil
Dorchester	Isle of Wight	St Neots	

Francis Frith
Pioneer Victorian Photographer

Francis Frith, founder of the world-famous photographic archive, was a complex and multi-talented man. A devout Quaker and a highly successful Victorian businessman, he was philosophical by nature and pioneering in outlook. By 1855 he had already established a wholesale grocery business in Liverpool, and sold it for the astonishing sum of £200,000, which is the equivalent today of over £15,000,000. Now in his thirties, and captivated by the new science of photography, Frith set out on a series of pioneering journeys up the Nile and to the Near East.

He was the first photographer to venture beyond the sixth cataract of the Nile. Africa was still the mysterious 'Dark Continent', and Stanley and Livingstone's historic meeting was a decade into the future. The conditions for picture taking confound belief. He laboured for hours in his wicker dark-room in the sweltering heat of the desert, while the volatile chemicals fizzed dangerously in their trays. Back in London he exhibited his photographs and was 'rapturously cheered' by members of the Royal Society. His reputation as a photographer was made overnight.

By the 1870s the railways had threaded their way across the country, and Bank Holidays and half-day Saturdays had been made obligatory by Act of Parliament. All of a sudden the working man and his family were able to enjoy days out, take holidays, and see a little more of the world.

With typical business acumen, Francis Frith foresaw that these new tourists would enjoy having souvenirs to commemorate their days out. For the next thirty years he travelled the country by train and by pony and trap, producing fine photographs of seaside resorts and beauty spots that were keenly bought by millions of Victorians. These prints were painstakingly pasted into family albums and pored over during the dark nights of winter, rekindling precious memories of summer excursions. Frith's studio was soon supplying retail shops all over the country, and by 1890 F Frith & Co had become the greatest specialist photographic publishing company in the world, with over 2,000 sales outlets, and pioneered the picture postcard.

Francis Frith had died in 1898 at his villa in Cannes, his great project still growing. By 1970 the archive he created contained over a third of a million pictures showing 7,000 British towns and villages.

Frith's legacy to us today is of immense significance and value, for the magnificent archive of evocative photographs he created provides a unique record of change in the cities, towns and villages throughout Britain over a century and more. Frith and his fellow studio photographers revisited locations many times down the years to update their views, compiling for us an enthralling and colourful pageant of British life and character.

We are fortunate that Frith was dedicated to recording the minutiae of everyday life. For it is this sheer wealth of visual data, the painstaking chronicle of changes in dress, transport, street layouts, buildings, housing and landscape that captivates us so much today, offering us a powerful link with the past and with the lives of our ancestors.

Computers have now made it possible for Frith's many thousands of images to be accessed almost instantly. The archive offers every one of us an opportunity to examine the places where we and our families have lived and worked down the years. Its images, depicting our shared past, are now bringing pleasure and enlightenment to millions around the world a century and more after his death. For further information visit: www.francisfrith.co.uk

FREE PRINT OF YOUR CHOICE

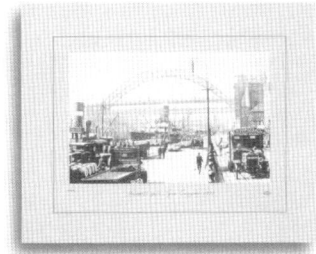

Mounted Print
Overall size 14 x 11 inches (355 x 280mm)

Choose any Frith photograph in this book.
Simply complete the Voucher opposite and return it with your remittance for £2.25 (to cover postage and handling) and we will print the photograph of your choice in SEPIA (size 11 x 8 inches) and supply it in a cream mount with a burgundy rule line (overall size 14 x 11 inches).
Please note: photographs with a reference number starting with a "Z" are not Frith photographs and cannot be supplied under this offer.
Offer valid for delivery to one UK address only.

PLUS: Order additional Mounted Prints at HALF PRICE - £7.49 each (normally £14.99)
If you would like to order more Frith prints from this book, possibly as gifts for friends and family, you can buy them at half price (with no additional postage and handling costs).

PLUS: Have your Mounted Prints framed
For an extra £14.95 per print you can have your mounted print(s) framed in an elegant polished wood and gilt moulding, overall size 16 x 13 inches (no additional postage and handling required).

IMPORTANT!

These special prices are only available if you use this form to order . You must use the ORIGINAL VOUCHER on this page (no copies permitted). We can only despatch to one UK address. This offer cannot be combined with any other offer.

Send completed Voucher form to:
The Francis Frith Collection, Frith's Barn, Teffont, Salisbury, Wiltshire SP3 5QP

CHOOSE A PHOTOGRAPH FROM THIS BOOK

Voucher for FREE and Reduced Price Frith Prints

Please do not photocopy this voucher. Only the original is valid, so please fill it in, cut it out and return it to us with your order.

Picture ref no	Page no	Qty	Mounted @ £7.49	Framed + £14.95	Total Cost £
		1	Free of charge*	£	£
			£7.49	£	£
			£7.49	£	£
			£7.49	£	£
			£7.49	£	£
			£7.49	£	£

Please allow 28 days for delivery.
Offer available to one UK address only

* Post & handling		£2.25
Total Order Cost		£

Title of this book . . . .

I enclose a cheque/postal order for £ . . . .
made payable to 'The Francis Frith Collection'

OR please debit my Mastercard / Visa / Maestro / Amex card, details below

Card Number

Issue No (Maestro only)   Valid from (Maestro)

Expires   Signature

Name Mr/Mrs/Ms . . . .
Address . . . .
. . . .
. . . .
. . . . Postcode . . . .
Daytime Tel No . . . .
Email . . . .

ISBN: 1-84567-748-X   Valid to 31/12/08